Gift of the Jaguar

John Franklin
with Sharon Franklin

ISBN: 0-615-27047-6
ISBN-13: 9780615270470

Visit www.booksurge.com to order additional copies.

To our son Francis Joseph,
whose life inspired us to follow our dreams.

Foreword

There is a place beyond mind, a different reality that can be accessed through experience, faith, and wisdom. Many people have an understanding of the ancient teachings of Peruvian culture, but only a few truly embody their essence in the way that John and Sharon do. *Gift of the Jaguar* takes us on a journey of initiation and self-discovery through the rugged landscape of fears and regrets. Guided by the profound wisdom of Andean shamans, we learn how to move through life with a sense of purpose and with connection to those who came before us and to those who will follow.

Dr. Theo Paredes, Founding Director of the Poqen Kanchay Foundation

Gift of the Jaguar is a hero's journey, Peruvian style. Carried by a strong current of writing, the story is educational and entertaining. I have traveled with John and Sharon and Dr. Paredes in Peru and am moved by the authentic feel of the characters and their way of life. The teachings of Dr. Paredes come through in a powerful way. And I am humbled by the way in which Zero Balancing becomes so real and obvious in a context outside of doing a session. The way in which the ideas behind this body-mind healing modality have been interwoven with Andean healing traditions highlights the principles of nature upon which Zero Balancing is built.

Gift of the Jaguar teaches much about the journey between life and death. The weaving of reality, dreams, and fantasies into the tapestry of Juan's journey is especially effective. I found myself going in and out of expanded states of consciousness as I traveled with him on his adventures. The energy of the Franklins' writing makes the story so real it is easy for me to believe that much of their book comes from personal experience. *Gift of the Jaguar* got me out of my left-brain, allowing me to enjoy so much meaningful material about ethics, healing, and life that I came away feeling a wiser, more clearly directed person. I think that this book will be extremely valuable for most readers, especially in the area of personal transformation.

Fritz Frederick Smith, M.D., Founder of Zero Balancing

Chapter One

Juan was wet with sweat when he awoke. He swallowed the bad feeling that rose up from his stomach and took a deeper breath. The fear that had stalked him in his sleep when he was little had never left but had only been hiding. It was his sister Marta and the day of the storm that haunted his dreams. This time she rode a black jaguar, and she was chasing him.

His father, Humberto, shook his shoulder a second time. He stared at Juan, the furrow deep between his thick eyebrows. "You're almost eighteen. I thought you were done with that," he muttered and walked away. Juan wanted to tell him that it wasn't his fault. If he could forget that day, he would. But it didn't work that way. Not if his father still blamed him for his sister's death.

His younger brother stirred beside him, pushing against a sister who nestled closer to their mother. Unaware of her children's jostling, Wilhelmita snored loudly. Juan slipped out from between the covers and tucked the edges of the alpaca blankets around his brother. He slid on his poncho and sandals in front of the oven. His eyes watered from the acrid gray haze that hung beneath the rafters of the thatched roof. Without a flue, more of the fire's heat stayed inside the stacked rock walls. So did the smoke from the burning of eucalyptus wood and dried dung gathered from their herd of llamas and alpacas.

He saw that his father's new poncho was stiff across his shoulders. Juan's mother had finished it last night. A few days in the fields on Inkawari Mountain would loosen up the tight weave. Humberto picked up a dented, blackened copper kettle and set it by the door. Juan grabbed it without saying anything and stepped outside.

The four stars of the Southern Cross and the Eyes of the Jaguar were still visible in the dark morning skies. He shivered in the cold air, but he took time to find the other constellations

1

fading over the distant peaks. It was his sister Marta who taught him to begin the day this way. She said there were sacred *apus* in the Andes of southern Peru that had their own star. Shamans traveled great distances to find one, she said. When Juan insisted that she take him to one of these special mountains, she laughed. Marta said he would have to wait until he was much older.

He heard a snort and turned toward the corral. The llama stamped her feet and flicked her ears toward Juan. Her dark head weaved back and forth above the wooden poles across the gate. It would be unlikely for a mountain lion to come this close to the village. But something had La Reina spooked. The rest of the llamas and alpacas circled behind her, their breath rising in the dry cold. He picked up a stick and walked around the perimeter of stacked rock that formed the rest of the corral. Robbed of the last few moments of sleep before dawn, two burros leaning into each other brayed in protest. The bony crossbred cow grabbed a few strands of hay left on the ground. Her calf tugged at her teats. Nothing seemed out of place.

Satisfied, he shrugged and dropped the stick. Kettle in hand, Juan turned up the path that meandered upstream along the river, away from the village. His father complained that he went too far for water, but it gave him a chance to be alone. He could watch for animals that came to the river. Mostly it was birds, but he'd seen foxes, deer, and an occasional mountain lion. Reaching the river, he knelt close to the water's edge and set the kettle down. A pair of torrent ducks studied him from the other side. The drake fluttered his wings nervously.

The image of Juan's face, the color of red clay, was lost in the dark eddies of Puma Rimac. He took a deep breath and stuck his hands into the river. The icy water stung when he washed, but the brisk rub with the edge of the wool poncho felt good. His eyes followed the dark blue sky tapered along the eastern edge of more distant mountains. The crest of Ausangate stood over the others of the Cordillera Vilcanota range, its snow-capped peaks silhouetted against the faint light of dawn. His sister had told him that this mountain had special powers and listened when you prayed. Storm clouds that hung heavy over its peaks the day she died must have kept it from hearing their prayers. Still he prayed because it was what his people had always done. He blew his breath over three coca leaves and tossed them onto the water. The swift current swept his offering downstream.

The torrent ducks were the only creatures that stirred this morning. The drake, talking in a series of low quacks, cautiously led the female toward the edge of the bank. It surprised Juan when one of them cried out, and they suddenly flapped their wings. The ducks flew in an arc across the river before they headed downstream. He looked back to the opposite shore. The tall grass on the other side stood motionless.

He grabbed the kettle and scooped it underneath the water. When one end of the handle slipped out from its bracket, he swung the kettle and landed it on the bank. The top of the grass on the other side rippled and then stopped. There wasn't any breeze this morning. He scanned the other side, but he couldn't see anything that moved. There was nothing there. He was starting to act like the llama. Maybe it was restless nestlings that the ducks had left behind. It wouldn't be long before his father wondered where the water for morning tea was. It was time to get back home.

He started to reach for the kettle, but the long-stemmed grass on the other side of the river trembled again. He was sure of it. He kept his eyes fixed on the opposite shore. Perhaps it was a mountain lion coming to the river for a drink. It could have been what the llama had smelled. He took his hand off the kettle and waited.

Dark as a moonless night, the beast slipped through the reeds. It looked up and down the bank before it stepped closer to the water. The rounded ears that swiveled around seemed too small for its massive head. It pointed its nose in the air and raised its lips. A pair of fangs that spanned the width of a man's head glistened in the dim light. It was no mountain lion, Juan realized.

It was a jaguar. And it was black. Just like the one his sister rode in his dream.

He had caught a glimpse of one in the jungle once, but its coat had been yellow with black splotches. He'd been picking coca leaves with his father, and the jaguar had been a brief flash between thick foliage. This one sat on the bank and scratched its side with a hind foot before it lowered its head to the water. The jaguar was most likely on its way back to the jungle and was just passing through. This could be the only chance that he'd ever have to see one this close. He watched the muscles ripple down its neck as it lapped the water.

Mountain lions were usually shy around people, but jaguars he wasn't sure about. He wrapped his fingers around the handle of the kettle and stepped backward in a crouch. When the other end of the handle came loose, the kettle banged against a rock. The jaguar raised its head, and it stared across the river. A low-throated growl froze Juan in place.

The river might discourage a mountain lion from crossing. But a jaguar could swim. It caught and ate caimans, the alligators that lived in the rivers of the jungle. And it ran down forest deer, delivering death with a single bite to the head. To kill with a single bite was what "jaguar" meant. His father had always told him not to run from a mountain lion, but to stand up and to look big. But Juan wasn't sure if the same held true for a jaguar.

The cat's front paws touched the water's edge. The sheen of dew darkened its black fur. Its broad nostrils flared, and its yellow eyes shone in the dim light. The jaguar growled, but Juan didn't dare look away. The fierce eyes forbade it. An image flashed inside his head. It was a young man huddled on the bank, a dented copper kettle by his foot. Stricken with fear, his dark eyes were dilated. It was him. He was seeing himself through the jaguar's eyes.

He stayed small and breathed invisible breaths. The sound of rushing water faded into the background. All time condensed into this moment. The beast, its menacing jaws opened, stepped into the river. When he saw the water at the cat's chest, he knew he had to run. The pounding inside his chest told him so. But he couldn't move. His feet were no longer under his control. It was like his dream. *Please Ausangate*, he prayed.

The jaguar raised its head and sniffed the air with an open mouth. Juan remembered what his father said. He had to stand. But before he could move, the black coat blended into the river, vanishing back into the darkness from which it had come. The jaguar had turned and swum downstream.

Juan stared at the water, hardly trusting his eyes. It was a close call, every fiber in his being stretched to its limit. He had to tell his father what he had just seen. No one had ever seen a jaguar this close to the village. The size of it would impress even him. But he would leave out the part about seeing through its eyes. His father would never believe that.

When the stones crunched behind him, the cold emptiness inside his stomach and the prickly feeling on his neck kept him from standing up. The beast that killed with a single bite must have crossed the stream. It had circled behind him. And it was too late to run. He slipped a fist-sized rock into his hand. When he spun around, his long arm released the stone with a fluid, hard snap.

His father grunted and dropped to his knees, clutching his groin. Juan stared with a mixture of disbelief, relief, and worry. The stiff poncho must have softened the rock's impact, he hoped. Humberto fell to his side, moaning. Curled in a ball, he rolled from side to side. It was painful to watch.

"Are you okay?" Juan asked.

His father had one hand underneath his poncho when he finally staggered up to his feet. The dim light made the scars from frostbite on his nose and his cheeks look harsh. Humberto grimaced when he saw the muddy spot on the front of his new poncho. His eyes held a smoldering edge. "What's the matter with you, boy? Have you lost your mind?" he said.

"You almost scared the life out of me," Juan said. "I thought you were a jaguar."

"A jaguar?"

He tried to meet his father's eyes but gave up and pointed across the river. "I saw a jaguar over there," he said. "It was black and it must have weighed close to three hundred pounds."

"Where?" asked Humberto. One eyebrow arched, but the rest of his face remained unchanged.

"In the middle over there." Juan waved his hand across the water. "And it started to cross the river before it headed downstream. It must have been what spooked La Reina this morning. At first I thought it might have been a mountain lion."

Humberto slowly scanned both sides of the river. Not even the top of the grass moved. He rubbed his hands across his face before he turned toward his son. Juan squirmed when the furrow between the thick eyebrows deepened. "There's nothing there now," his father said. "I've never seen a jaguar this far from the jungle. And it's rare to catch a glimpse even there, especially a black one."

"But..."

Humberto looked back across the river. "It was likely a puma. In the dark, it would be hard to tell. Still, a puma this close to the village is not good. Most likely, it was an old one, unable to hunt much, and maybe looking for an easy meal. Keep a close eye on the herd today. I'll tell the others to be on the lookout also."

Juan stood up and met his father's stare. "I know the difference between a jaguar and a mountain lion. It was a jaguar," he said.

Humberto's eyebrows almost touched. His face flushed an even darker shade before he answered. He glanced down at the kettle lying on its side. "Your mother will worry if you're not back soon," he said. "She was working on breakfast when I left the house." His father turned to leave but stopped. "There's one other thing. You'll have company today. Rosa asked if you could help move her grandfather's herd to the upper pastures," he said.

He looked away from his father. He couldn't help it. He didn't want him to see his face. Just her name made him blush.

Without further explanation, Humberto turned and walked stiffly back toward the village. Juan grabbed the kettle and pushed it back under the water. Curling his dark toenails into the hard leather of his sandals, he fixed his eyes on the ground. If his father had seen how big that creature was, he would understand that it couldn't have been a mountain lion. He looked up. The tracks, he thought. The jaguar would have left tracks on the other side.

The slip of daylight along the eastern edge of the mountains would be enough. He ran along the water until he reached the shallow ford downstream where the herds crossed on their way to the high pasture. Juan ran back up the other side of the river until he reached the place where he had seen the jaguar. He pushed away the branches of a woody bush and stepped carefully through the tall grass still coated with early morning ice crystals. A tuft of black hair clung to one of the broken stems. He slowly spread the grass apart. There in the moist earth were the jaguar's footprints. Even when he spread his fingers out, his hand fit inside one paw print. The tracks were bigger than a mountain lion's. He traced the track with the tip of his index finger before he saw the pricks in the dirt several inches away. The claws had to have been huge. Juan realized that he had overlooked a more important detail. The jaguar could still be there.

The brush was thick, and it was impossible for him to see more than a few feet. It could have circled back. He'd heard how a jaguar might lie in wait to ambush its prey. It could be hidden in the brush at this very moment, its tail twitching, ready to puncture his skull with a single bite. He stayed low and edged backward toward the bank. His foot slipped against the mud before he could grab onto the branches of the bush. The leaves tore off in his hands, and he fell into the freezing water, hitting his ribs against the sharp edge of a rock. The current tugged at the woolen poncho and dragged him along the bottom. He gasped for air whenever his mouth broke the surface. Half floating and half swimming, he pulled himself from one rock to the next until he crawled up to the other side of Puma Rimac.

Juan went back to where he'd left the kettle. He looked across. The grass might have moved, but he couldn't be sure. He grabbed the kettle and headed home. His side ached with each step, but he didn't slow down. He had to tell his father about the tracks before he left for the fields. He took a shortcut and came up behind the corral. The llamas and alpacas jostled against each another. One of the burros kicked, barely missing the calf. Juan shouted at it before he turned toward the house. He didn't see Rosa until it was too late.

Chapter Two

Rosa stumbled backward when Juan bumped her shoulder, but she managed to catch his arm. Water splashed over the top of the kettle onto her. His face flushed when he saw the laughter in the cinnamon brown eyes. He stepped back. "I didn't see you coming. Sorry about the water," he mumbled.

She shook off her many-layered woolen skirt and glanced up at him. It had been a while since they had said more than hello. "It's okay," she said. Her eyes lingered on his clothes. She looked at the puddle at his feet and chewed on her lower lip. "You went for a swim?" she asked. Half of her lower lip didn't lift when she smiled. It had been that way since she was born. Rosa covered her mouth. She was trying hard not to laugh.

"I was running and I slipped," he said.

"Running?"

"Never mind," he said.

"I've been looking for you."

Juan tried to ignore the knot in his stomach. They had been best friends when they were children. They'd followed his sister around the village and played in her make-believe stories. But Marta's death had ended that. He clenched his teeth to keep them from chattering. His ears tingled on their way to numbness.

Rosa's black eyebrows rose. "Are you all right?" she said. "You must be freezing. You'd best get inside."

A high-pitched voice rang out from inside the stone walls of the house. It was his mother, and she didn't sound happy.

"I'm okay," he said. "What do you want?"

"Your father said that you would help me with my grandfather's animals," she said. "The neighbor boy usually takes care of them, but he's going to Paucartambo with his father. It's been a while since I've done it." The tip of her tongue played with the rough edge of a chipped front tooth. Juan couldn't help but notice. He was reading her lips.

An angry voice rose from inside the house. It was his father.

"I've got to go now," Juan said. "Wait for me at the ford with your animals, and we'll go from there."

Rosa's eyes caught his discomfort. "Sure," she replied. "I'll see you later." She tossed her braid behind her and spun around. Juan watched her walk away before he stepped toward the front door.

His mother's voice waxed and waned in a singsong rhythm. "You know that it was a jaguar, Humberto," she said. "The only reason that you told Juan it was a puma was because of what the shaman said."

"What are you talking about?" he asked.

Juan set the kettle down outside the house and tucked his hands underneath his armpits. His sodden clothes held the cold close against his skin. He shivered and tried not to think about the fire on the other side of the door.

"You know good and well what I'm talking about," his mother said. "Don Francisco said it would be a black jaguar that came for our son."

"No, Wilhelmita," he said. "There's no reason to even be talking about that. Not now, not ever. I don't care what that old man told you. He had his own purposes in mind, not what's best for us or our son. Juan will be a farmer like me and like my father and all the Del Gatos before him. Haven't you heard a word I've been saying?"

Juan felt the awkward silence settle in the room on the other side of the door. His mother had been deaf since she was five. It was the scarlet fever, his father had told him. Reading lips was the only way that she could understand what others said. He heard Humberto clear his throat before he spoke again. His voice was lower, almost apologetic.

"He's seventeen, almost eighteen years old," he said. "He should be thinking about his future. But his mind hasn't been on work lately, that's for sure. Even when he ought to be swinging a hoe, I'll turn around and see him leaning on it.

He watched eagles circle overhead yesterday with such yearning
on his face that you would have thought he was six years old."

"Why does that surprise you? You had to know that things
would be different for him." His mother's voice trembled.
"Where is he? I thought you said that he was coming."

"He's probably looking for tracks along the river," Humberto
said. "That'd be just like him. I'll tell you what his problem
is. He just needs to concentrate more. And you need to stop
treating him like a child. He's got to do more than turn eighteen
to be a man in this house."

His words pierced Juan's chest. He wished that he'd never
seen the jaguar. One of his little sisters began to cry. His father
told her to hush and to go back to sleep.

"Besides, Wilhelmita, he's always had problems," Humberto
said. "For years after Marta died, he had those bad dreams. Just
this morning he was tossing and calling her name. I had to wake
him so that he wouldn't bother the others."

Juan swore under his breath at the mention of his sister's
name. He couldn't help it if she still haunted his dreams.

"Just give him some time," his mother said. "Besides, the coca
leaves don't lie, not in Don Francisco's hands. When he saw that
scar in our son's hand, he spoke of the condor. Someday our son
would be called to walk the shaman's path, he said." Her voice
trailed off.

"He's my son, and he needs to keep his mind on farming,"
Humberto said. "In a few days, the village will be giving him his
own land to work. That's what's important. And that's what we
need to be thinking about, not the prophecy of a foolish old man."

Wilhelmita's whisper carried a harsh edge. "There was a time
when you told a different story. You were the one that wanted to
be a healer. Don't let bitterness cloud your vision. That shaman
said a lot more to me that day. He told me not to let Juan go with
his sister and the herd until he turned seven. And I warned you.
If you had listened to me then, Marta might still be alive."

"You shut up about that, Wilhelmita. You hear me?"

The room fell quiet. The knot in Juan's stomach made him
feel like he'd swallowed something dry and hard. At least the

fighting was over. He stomped his feet and knocked the mud off his sandals before he stepped inside. He pulled the door shut and walked past his father.

His mother leaned over the adobe oven. Her hair, streaked with gray, still needed to be braided. The white fringe around the brim of her hat shook. She jumped when Juan hung the kettle over the fire. Wet lines ran down her cheeks. Her eyes widened and thick lips parted around teeth stained dark from a lifetime of chewing coca. She touched her fingers to his face.

"Are you all right?" she asked. "Your father said that…" Humberto tapped her shoulder. Wilhelmita jumped and looked back over her shoulder at him.

"There's no need to talk about that anymore," he said. "Let the boy tell us why he's soaked."

She hushed him with a wave of her hand and turned back to Juan. Her eyes were crossed, straining to read his lips. The smell of garlic was strong on her breath. "What happened?" she said. "Did the jaguar chase you into the river? Is that how come you're wet?" The high-pitched warble in her voice broke, giving her words a raw sound.

His father stared at him. Juan shrugged his shoulders and looked down. He shouldn't have been so careless, he realized. It could have been worse, much worse. "Not exactly," he said. "It was an accident." Humberto walked out the door, his bag and hoe slung over his shoulder.

"Take those clothes off and come stand next to the fire," said his mother. "You're shivering." She took the sodden hat and poncho and his shirt from him and pulled a blanket around his shoulders. "We don't need anyone else in this family sick."

"He must be really mad," Juan said. "He didn't even take his lunch."

"Don't worry," she said. "Your sisters can carry it to him. The important thing is that you're okay." She wrapped her heavy arms around him, squeezing his elbow hard against his bruised ribs. When he twisted to the side, his mother pulled the blanket away from his chest.

Juan winced when she probed around the injury. He kept the blanket wrapped around his waist and stared into the fire. Wilhelmita grabbed a pot of salve made from *maych'a* leaves and smeared a thin layer over the abraded skin. She wrapped a strip of cloth over it and made several passes around his chest before she tied the ends of the bandage together.

A thin ribbon of steam rose from the kettle and blended into air already heavy with smoke. Wilhelmita pulled out a handful of coca leaves from a feed sack on the floor and dropped them into the kettle. Juan touched her shoulder with a light hand, but she still jumped. He shaped his lips deliberately when she looked at him. "Why didn't you tell me about Don Francisco's reading of the leaves?" he asked.

His mother stared at his lips, the web-like lines deepening in her face. Her chest sagged and her eyes grew wistful. "I wasn't supposed to tell you. Your father was furious when I tried to tell him. He said nothing good could come of it. After that day of the storm, I began to think that he was right." Her calloused hand patted his cheek. "Don't be angry with me. I've only wanted what's best for you," she said.

Juan knew that there was more than she was telling him. "Why does Papá hate that shaman? Is it because of what he said about me?"

"It's more than that," she replied. "We'll talk about it another time. I wish you could have known your father when he was your age. But things happened." She wiped her eyes with her apron. "I know that his talk is rough, but he wants what's best for you."

Someone knocked on the door and shouted. Clutching the blanket around him, Juan walked over and opened it. A woman from the village stood there with a puzzled look on her face. "Usually one of your sisters lets me in," she said. "I'm here to talk with Wilhelmita. She told me that this morning would be a good time." He translated her words with his lips to his mother.

She shook her head. "Tell her that I'm busy now," she said silently. "She'll have to come back this afternoon." The woman nodded when he told her and left.

Wilhelmita grabbed the kettle and filled his cup. The littlest girl, the one who had been crying earlier, pulled on her mother's skirts. Wilhelmita lifted her up to her hip and turned her attention back to the oven. "Did you see Rosa?" She looked over her shoulder. "Juanito?" He stared at the leaves in the bottom of his cup. He nodded, but he didn't look up. "And?" He glanced at her face, but he avoided meeting her eyes. His other little sister tugged at her skirts and waited to be picked up. His mother broke off a piece of potato and gave it to her.

"She told me about her grandfather's herd," he said.

"He's getting on in years, and he depends on Rosa a lot," Wilhelmita said. "I'm happy that she asked for your help." She waited until Juan looked at her again. "You know, she always makes a special effort to stop and visit with me. Sometimes when your father and you are in the fields, she'll spend the whole morning here. We'll sit outside and do our weaving together and just talk. She doesn't have any trouble understanding me. And your sisters adore her."

He grabbed the dry clothes that his mother held out. Wilhelmita turned back to the oven but kept talking. "She's such a nice girl and very pretty, yes, Juanito? And her parents are good people." She glanced back at him, and he rushed to pull up the pair of pants over his waist. Juan knew where this was going.

"I know," he said.

"There's the dance at the Farmer's Festival," she said. Her voice dropped to a whisper. "Rosa's waiting for you to ask her, but don't tell her that I told you. Today would be the perfect time for you to talk with her." Juan grabbed an old, threadbare poncho and pulled it over his head. "I can remember when you were little, and you walked around the village holding her hand. There was no keeping you apart."

Wilhelmita went over to check on José when he stuck his head out from underneath the blankets and coughed repeatedly. Juan grabbed a handful of potatoes from the oven. He burned his fingers and almost dropped some on the floor before he could stuff them into his bag. He grabbed his brother's hat and a water

14

pouch off the hook by the door. He waved and pulled the door shut without looking back at his mother.

It should have been his brother's job to graze the herd, but José had come home sick with a fever yesterday. His mother had put him in bed and insisted that Juan take over until his brother felt better. The herd had been his job before he was old enough to work with his father in the fields. But today would be different. There was a black jaguar out there somewhere, and he'd be responsible for two herds. If they forded the Puma Rimac farther downstream, he and Rosa could drive the animals to the high pastures that stretched between Inkawari and Ausangate mountains. They would be unlikely to have any problems there with all the other herds around. Besides, jaguars only hunted at night, he thought.

La Reina stretched her long neck over the wooden poles of the gate. Her round, dark eyes seemed to understand his concern. The llama pushed her warm muzzle against his face, and he scratched her forehead. "Soon enough, you'll be eating grass to your heart's content," he said. At least he wouldn't have to worry about his parents for a while. He didn't know which was worse, a father that wouldn't listen or a mother that talked too much. And both thinking they knew what was best for him.

Then there was Rosa. He must have looked like a fool this morning, standing there dripping wet and freezing half to death. And if that wasn't enough, his parents had argued loud enough for the whole village to hear.

La Reina snorted in his ear. "Not you too," he sputtered. Juan wiped the slobber off the side of his face and grabbed the rope halter. With red tasseled ears and a tinkling brass bell around her neck, the black llama stepped out of the corral and onto the path toward the river. He whistled and swung his *huaraca* behind the rest of the herd, tapping the woven slingshot against the burros' flanks to hasten their grudging pace.

Maybe he should talk to Rosa about the dance. Of course, there were other boys always around her, laughing and carrying on. But that wasn't the worst of it. It was the talking to her. A lot had been left unsaid between them over the years since

Marta had died. It might be best to leave it that way. Juan shouted at one of the burros that had stopped to graze. He slipped a rock into his woolen sling. The indignant burro brayed and kicked up its rear legs when the stone bounced off its backside, and then it trotted toward the rest of the herd.

Chapter Three

A smoky haze had drifted over the village by the time he reached the river. Men dotted the face of Inkawari Mountain, harvesting the patchwork of steep fields that Juan had helped to plant. Springtime patches of white and purple flowers had produced a variety of small but hardy dark and light-skinned potatoes. They'd come from stocks cultivated by their ancestors from a single wild plant native to southern Peru, his father had told him. The stone walls that terraced the hillsides and the irrigation channels carved from rock had once been part of a vast Inca civilization. The Incas knew how to fit stones that were the height of three men together with joints so fine that not a drop of mortar was needed. The massive temple walls found in ancient sites like Machu Picchu could still withstand powerful earthquakes, Humberto told him.

But after the Conquest, the King of Spain deeded the land to wealthy owners who built haciendas and made the people work for them. It had been that way for hundreds of years, even after Peru won its independence. But now the people of San Mateo owned the land, at least those who had reached the age of eighteen.

He was thirteen when he first worked with his father in the fields. Humberto led the oxen, and he'd followed behind. In the beginning, the plow slung him from side to side, leaving uneven cuts in the ground. Over time, he'd learned to handle the wooden pole with a single blade so that it split the dark clay soil into straight furrows. "It's important to do it right," his father had said. "Someday it will be yours. If a man is willing to work hard, the land will take care of him and his family."

Juan had worked hard to measure up to his father over the past five years. And in three days, the day of his eighteenth birthday, the village would give him his own land. Juan Eduardo Del Gato would be a man. He wondered if a man should still have bad dreams.

High up on the other side of the river, a cloud of dust rose from a well-worn path winding its way up to the high pastures. He frowned when he saw the black braid plaited with red yarn that swung behind the burgundy sweater. Rosa must have gotten tired of waiting and decided to move her grandfather's herd by herself. She knew that it would be less work to graze the animals closer to the village. Latecomers would have to go farther out onto the grasslands.

His herd crowded into the water, scattering the pair of torrent ducks and newly hatched ducklings. The brass bell around La Reina's neck jingled amidst hoof beats across the rocky ford. The strands of crimson yarn waved from the tips of her ears. The bull calf bawled behind his mother. The two burros snatched mouthfuls of grass between Juan's shouts and his waving slingshot.

The sun had climbed high into a blue sky dotted with clouds when he and the animals crested the plateau. The hardy yellow *ichu* rippled in undulating waves. Other herds already dotted the grassland that stretched across the bed of an ancient inland sea, its distant edges lapping against rocky foothills. The sunlight reflected off the glacier-capped mountains of the Cordillera Vilcanota range that towered over the *altiplano*. Scattered clouds drifted over the peaks of Ausangate.

He wiped his brow and took a swallow of water. Juan was seven when he first brought the herd by himself. His mother had come with him at the beginning. Gradually, he lost his fear of storms and had learned to enjoy the solitude. He practiced with his slingshot until he had gotten good enough to take down an occasional rabbit-like vizcacha. The best part was that he hadn't had to talk to anyone else, except for Don Francisco. It was the shaman who had taught him how to read the clouds.

When he saw the burgundy sweater moving toward a distant knoll, he dropped the water pouch down to his side, waved his hands, and shouted at the animals. Gray pocket gophers disappeared into shallow holes with cries that sounded like their names, tuco-tucos. He skirted the herd past the *puna* plants with sword-like leaves and long thorns and managed to keep the calf away from the mounds of stones and sticks that ringed the burrows of the vizcachas.

When he caught up with Rosa, the sun was at midday. Sweat plastered the hair hanging out from underneath his hat against his face. He slapped the dust from his wool poncho. She had found a good stand of grass. And the boulders at the top of the knoll that overlooked the herd promised afternoon shade.

He took in the graceful curves underneath the alpaca sweater. Layers of a colorful skirt tapered to a snug fit around her slender waist. Rosa Maria Q'espi was no longer a little girl in spiked pigtails.

Their long necks swiveling nervously, the alpacas and llamas parted around him. La Reina dropped her head to tear a bite out of the tough *ichu*. When dust funnels spun across the knoll, she jerked her head up and snorted. The brass bell tinkled when the black llama shook her neck and stamped her foot. He studied the jumbled mass of gray rocks on top. Juan didn't realize that he'd seen La Reina's back from the higher vantage point until later. Finally, after the wind quieted, she dropped her head and started to graze again.

Seeing nothing, he continued to walk toward Rosa. She kept her eyes fixed on the mountains. Her hands were wrapped around a walking stick. Her thick black eyebrows rose with an amused look when he stood in front of her.

"You were supposed to wait for me," he said. "I told you that I'd help you with your herd."

Her brow wrinkled further underneath the old brown felt hat that she wore. She moistened her lips and gave him that half-smile. "Thanks, but I did okay by myself," she said.

Moments passed with only the sound of wind blowing across the rocky knoll. Scratching through his hat, Juan watched La Reina for few moments. He turned back to Rosa. "I saw a jaguar this morning on the upper part of Puma Rimac."

"I heard that it was a puma," she said. "That's what your father told me before I ran into you this morning. Or before you ran into me." Her half-smile widened.

"It was a black jaguar, not a mountain lion," Juan insisted.

She arched one eyebrow. Her expression caught him off guard. A slow burn crept up his neck and spread across his face. He dropped his eyes and pulled a burr off the cuff of his pants. He looked back at his herd. The cow and her calf had drifted away from the rest of the animals.

"There's plenty of grass here for both herds," Rosa said. "You can run your animals with mine if you like."

"Well fine then," he muttered and walked back toward the strays. He had half a mind to take his animals somewhere else to graze.

He grabbed the rope around the cow's neck. Rosa screamed. The cow snorted and almost took his arm off with a sudden twist of her head. Juan jumped out of the way and looked back. The jaguar's leap from the top of the boulders seemed to unfold in slow motion. The llama's haunches twisted sideways with a loud crack when the three-hundred-pound cat landed on her back. Unable to stand, La Reina's hooves flailed against the rocks. The cow's clanging bell, her calf's bawling, and the donkeys' braying erupted amidst drumming hooves. Alpaca and llama necks crisscrossed in a dozen different directions, swaying back and forth with each stride.

With its small, rounded ears flattened against its head and its mouth open, the jaguar hung onto the llama. Its front claws dug into her neck and slashed through the veins nestled in deep furrows. Its hind legs raked her flanks, slashing open dark red streaks of muscle. Splashes of crimson darkened the black coats of both animals. The cat snarled and spit, exposing its yellow fangs, and clamped its massive jaws around the sides of the llama's head. It pierced her skull with a grisly crunch. La Reina shuddered and lay still.

Juan shouted at Rosa and ran toward her. She was waving her stick. He grabbed her arm and pulled her away, but her foot caught on a rock and she fell against him. Off balance, his feet slipped in the loose shale, and he landed on the ground with her on top. A deep growl brought an eerily sudden stillness to the confusion. Juan rolled to the side and sprang up onto his hands and knees. His gaze shot upward.

Irregular squiggles traced a faint mosaic of rosettes over the jaguar's black coat. Taut, compact muscles rippled across its deep chest. It dropped the llama's head from its mouth and fixed its eyes on Juan.

The pictures were back inside Juan's head, but they came too fast. *Stand*, a voice said. *Now*. He slipped his *huaraca* from around his waist and slid a stone inside the pouch. With his eyes on the jaguar, he stood slowly onto his feet. He choked back the bad feeling that hung in his throat. Neither he nor Rosa would see this day end, he feared. The jaguar would kill them both.

The cat raised its lip and flattened back its ears. The angle of the sun shining into its eyes tightened its pupils into black dots. Blood matted the fur around its jowls and ran down its neck and chest in dark ridges. The jaguar shifted its weight onto its hind legs. Juan felt cold and hollow. Only the lifeless body of the llama and scant rocky ground separated him from the beast. He had but one chance with the rope-like sling. He had to be quick, and he had to be lucky. A shot between the eyes could stun it just long enough for them to escape. If the jaguar lunged first, his life would end the way that La Reina's had. But Rosa could still make it.

"Stay behind me and step back slowly," he whispered to her without taking his eyes off the cat. "Keep going and don't look back, no matter what."

The jaguar's deep throated growl vibrated through Juan's chest. Its fangs, chiseled by a lifetime of crunching bones, were stained with fresh kill. Drops of bloody saliva hung bead-like on its whiskers. When the beast locked its yellow eyes onto his, Juan saw a man's face masked by sweat-streaked dirt and eyes made fierce by desperation. It was his face. A *huaraca* hung by his side, his knuckles white around the sling. Rosa stood next to him, her staff clutched across her chest.

The cat shifted its weight to its front legs and shook its head. It clamped its jaws around the llama's head and scrambled up the rocks, dragging the carcass behind. The tinkle of the llama's brass bell carried in the wind, and then it fell quiet.

Covered with gray dust, Rosa looked like a ghost. Sweat traced muddy paths across her brow and down her cheeks. She pointed her finger toward the boulders. The trail of blood, congealed into dark, dirty streaks on the yellow grass, disappeared at the top of the knoll. Her knees sagged. Juan grabbed her before she fell. She hung onto his arms and her head fell against his chest. He wrapped his arms around her, not knowing if it was enough or too much. He had never held a girl before, not like this. When he felt her move, he didn't know if he should still keep his arms around her. She dropped her hands to his waist and rested her head against his shoulder. Her breath was warm and smelled of the mint-like *muña*. She wiped her face on his sleeve.

"I'm sorry," Rosa said. "I've never seen anything like that before. That jaguar broke La Reina's back, and it crushed her skull like it was an egg. I felt so helpless. I know it's only a single breath and a heartbeat between life and death. I help my grandfather when people make their crossing. And I see babies that even Doña Mariana can't save. But with that jaguar, it was different. One moment La Reina was grazing and now only bloodstains are left on the ground where she stood. Your mother will be heartbroken," she said. "That llama meant the world to her."

His mother wouldn't be the only one who missed her. La Reina was his friend. She had always been there to listen to him. But he couldn't tell Rosa what he saw. The image of the llama's back from the top of the knoll was something that only the jaguar could have seen. How could he have seen it too? Hopefully the black cat would head back to the jungle, but he couldn't be certain. They had to let the other herders know about the jaguar. He heard the braying donkeys and shouts that carried in the swirling winds. He took Rosa by the arm, and they picked their way through the yellow *ichu* to find their animals.

Chapter Four

It was late in the afternoon when they came down from the
pastures and into the streets of San Mateo. The dust coated
people and animals with a gray pallor. The children pushed
the herds down the streets with shouts and whistles. Juan drove
theirs from behind, and Rosa kept the lead animals together.
The women watched from doorways with babies in their arms
and toddlers that hung onto their skirts. Driving the herd past
the houses, he ignored the stares of the worried mothers and
the fingers of children that pointed toward him. Juan heard the
word "jaguar" rise above the din in excited conversations.

He ached with tiredness. It was worse than if he'd worked
with his father all day. The cow and her calf and the burros
hadn't gone far, but it took most of the afternoon for him and
Rosa to separate out their llamas and alpacas from the other
herds. Once they were finished, it was easy to convince the
children to drive all the animals back to the village.

That jaguar was no ordinary one, Juan told the children. But
he didn't tell them all of it. He could hardly believe it himself.
He shuddered when he thought about La Reina's death. Two
close calls with the black jaguar were enough. He had to find out
what his mother knew about Don Francisco's reading of the coca
leaves. Next time he might not be so lucky.

Rosa turned the herd toward the house ahead. He knew
where she was going. And he knew who she would tell first about
the jaguar. She would tell her grandfather, whom she trusted
more than anyone. And Don Francisco would take in every word.
Then the shaman would want to talk with him.

He and Rosa had sat often with his sister Marta at the fire
in Don Francisco's home and listened to his stories about
their ancestors. These wisdom keepers still lived at the top

of Apu Ausangate with the mystical jaguar Otorongo, he told them. Afterward, Marta would take him and Rosa to a hill that overlooked the village. She and Rosa untied their braids and pretended to be the ancient ones whose black hair hung to their waists. Juan played the part of Otorongo. But that was a long time ago. What happened with that jaguar today was no children's story.

Rosa's whistle caught his attention. She shouted at him to drive the herd into the corral, and then she disappeared again, her braid swinging against her dirty sweater. He waved his arms and pushed the animals forward. It had been a while since he had talked with Don Francisco. When he was a boy and tending the herd, he would see him out on the high pastures. The shaman would gather the weedy *muña*, the shrub-like *maych'a* with yellow flowers, nettles, and other plants. Juan would hear his guttural chants rise in the gusting winds, but he could never figure out what the old man sang. When he saw him sing to a San Pedro cactus one day, he got up his nerve and asked him. Don Francisco told him that he sought the plant's blessing so that he could cut a piece from it. The San Pedro had a strong spirit, and it made a powerful tea for vision, he said.

After that, Juan helped him collect the cactus and other plants. The shaman taught him that *muña* was good for mental alertness and for digestion, and *maych'a* made a good poultice for hoof abscesses. He had showed him the best way to treat an infected umbilical cord, and he taught him how to make a salve from *maych'a* for an inflamed teat on a cow's udder. Juan had laughed when he told him about nettles. Used in a tea, it helped old men like him to pee better, he said. They talked about the weather, how to read the clouds, and how to know when a storm might come and which way it would travel. But they never talked about his sister Marta, and he was grateful for that. After he started to work with his father, he had seen little of the shaman.

With ears flattened against long, weaving necks, the llamas and alpacas snorted and jostled against each other. The burros brayed and twitched their tails in an angry tempo. They kept their back feet cocked at threatening angles toward a barking dog that appeared out of nowhere. The cow shook her horns and kept her bawling calf on the other side of her. When the herd turned the corner, Juan saw the wizened, bow-legged man with a staff in his hand. White hair hung beneath a brown felt hat, and an eagle feather dangled over the brim. It was Don Francisco. He stood in front of the corral built onto the side of his house, and he raised the staff over his head with both hands. A black poncho slid over thin, sinewy arms that were more bone than flesh.

Juan shouted for him to step aside. He'd drive the herd into the corral from behind. But the shaman stood there with his staff held high. The animals in the lead fidgeted and tried to stop, but the others pushed them forward. The herd circled and shoved themselves tighter against the middle. It was when the animals finally came to a standstill that Juan heard the strange lullaby that drifted over the herd. It was mournful and soothing at the same time.

Don Francisco dropped his arms. Juan strained to read the old man's lips when he spoke. His words were simple, but the tone of his voice was like a warm poultice. It was okay, he told the animals. The beast had not come for them. The animals in front pricked their ears and smacked their lips together. When they lowered their heads, it was an up and down nod that suggested a mutual consent. Even the dog stopped barking. When the shaman stepped inside the corral, the herd followed behind him. The burros, llamas, and alpacas, and the cow and her calf staked out their claims to the handfuls of cut grass scattered against the rock walls of the corral. Juan watched Don Francisco look over the animals. His movements were more cat-like than those of an old man.

The silence hung awkwardly between them when the shaman came over and stood next to him. Don Francisco's age was more apparent when the sunlight caught his face. A bluish haze from years of Andean sun and wind covered his eyes. His broad face was a craggy mountain, crisscrossed with wrinkles. He held onto a dark wooden staff with a claw-like grip and grabbed a rough-hewn eucalyptus pole with his other hand. Juan picked up the other end and slid it across the gate. He put up the rest of the poles by himself. When he heard Rosa's voice behind him, he slapped the dust off his poncho and pushed his bangs underneath his hat. Her face, freshly scrubbed, and her clean sweater and smile made her look radiant.

"Abuelito," she greeted Don Francisco. Her lips moved too fast near her grandfather's ear for Juan to understand what she said. The shaman held her hand and nodded quietly until she finished. He stepped in front of Juan. With his head tilted and eyes shielded by half-closed lids, Don Francisco began to hum.

A shadow spread over the ground in front of Juan. His eyelids flickered and his chin dropped. Time slowed to a barely perceptible crawl. The noise from the animals faded into the background. When the shaman blew a thin mist of perfumed water into his face and tapped the end of the staff against his chest, Juan grunted and stumbled backward. He could have sworn that he'd seen the silhouette of a jaguar leap into the shadow. But the shadow was gone.

He looked at Rosa's grandfather. "What did you do?" he said.

Don Francisco spoke in such a low voice that Juan had to read his lips to understand what he said. "You carry a lot of fear about the jaguar, but you needn't worry. Otorongo takes only those whose time has come." The shaman gave him an odd look before he added, "You saw more than you wanted. It scares you to see in this way. But you need to let your mother see that you're okay. Tell her that I'm sorry about La Reina."

The old man turned to Rosa and shrugged his shoulders. "We'll see," her grandfather said. "Come back later and we'll talk. I've got other things to do now."

Juan watched the shaman walk toward the squatty stone house tucked underneath the uneven thatched roof. "What was that about?" he asked.

Rosa waited until her grandfather disappeared through the doorway. The weathered door, tilted to one side, was left open. "I don't know, Juanito. He has his ways. Like he said, we'll see."

Juan rubbed his hand across his chest. He wondered if there was something that she wasn't telling him. Her eyes held the same funny look that her grandfather's did a moment ago. "About what?" he said. "What did you say to your grandfather?"

"I told my grandfather that we need to talk with him."

"I've got to go," Juan said. "My mother will be worried sick when she hears about the jaguar. And La Reina's death won't make it any easier. Our story is probably spreading like wind-driven fire. People will say that it was some old mountain lion that I should have been able to drive away."

"It was a jaguar, not a puma," Rosa said. "And what happened to the llama wasn't your fault." She rested her hands on his shoulders. "You stood and faced that jaguar, Juanito." Her brown eyes stirred up feelings that made him want to wrap his arms around her again, but Don Francisco was staring at him from inside the doorway.

Juan cleared his throat. "People are going to be pretty nervous for a while," he said. "I imagine that most will keep their herds close to the village until things calm down. But we can still graze our herds together. Meet me at the river in the morning, and we'll go up from there." He saw the funny look in Rosa's eyes again. "If it's okay with you," he added.

A half-smile crossed her lips. "I'll see you tomorrow," she said.

The lengthening shadows of the afternoon sun covered the streets by the time he had pushed the last burro into his family's corral. When he rounded the corner of the house, he saw that the door hung open. It was too late. His little sisters sat in the corner with their arms wrapped around each other. Wilhelmita's face was buried in her apron and her heavy shoulders trembled. His brother patted her back and tried to soothe her. When José saw Juan at the door, he tugged at his mother's arm. "Don't cry. He's okay," he said.

Wilhelmita rocked back and forth with her hands tucked under her arms, but she didn't get up at first. With his brother's wet nose on his neck and his sisters' arms around his legs, Juan reached out toward her. She was like this for months after Marta died. Wilhelmita grabbed onto him, and he helped her to stand up. It took time for the confusion and pain etched in her face to give way to relief. He formed his words with barely a sound when he caught her eyes. "I'm okay, and Rosa is too," he said.

His mother's voice cracked between uneven breaths when she spoke. "One of the neighbors told us that a jaguar had attacked you and Rosa. She left to get your father. We've been waiting, but we hadn't heard anything. I didn't want the children see you like...I thought that..." Her lips trembled and her hands shook, but she kept her eyes glued to Juan's face. "Rosa is okay?"

"She's fine, but the jaguar killed La Reina. She never had a chance," he said.

His mother squeezed his hand. She looked past him, through the open door. Her words made a hoarse warble. "Your grandmother used to say that when one is taken, another is spared. La Reina's death was her gift to you. Her mother was a gift from a dear friend when I was a young girl. She was the first animal that I ever owned. When La Reina was born, I gave her to your sister. She was to be the foundation of her herd when she got married." Wilhelmita dropped Juan's hand and gathered the girls under her arms.

The sun was still above the mountains when he saw Humberto running toward the house, his hoe over his shoulder. Maria and Anna hurried through the door, pushing against each other, and ran to meet him. Maybe he should talk with Rosa's grandfather. It was Don Francisco who foretold the jaguar's coming. If that beast was here because of his sister Marta, he would need the shaman's help. His life might depend on it.

Chapter Five

With the herd bunched between him and the river, Juan watched the ducks on the other side. The drake stepped out from the tall grass first, and then the ducklings, followed by the mother, moved cautiously toward the water. Juan sucked the juice from the wad of coca leaves in his cheek pouch. The grumbling of his stomach reminded him that he'd slipped out of the house without breakfast. His mother's deep sighs and sagging shoulders had been too much to bear this morning.

The furrow between his father's eyebrows had deepened and his mouth had set in a tight line when Juan told him about the jaguar last night. When he had asked him what would make a jaguar wander this far from the jungle, Humberto shrugged his shoulders and said that it would be best to keep the herd close to the village for the next few days. Juan had decided it was best not to upset him with any more questions. Besides, Don Francisco knew a lot more about that jaguar than he'd shared yesterday. Rosa's grandfather knew that he had seen through the jaguar's eyes. But Juan knew that he couldn't talk to the shaman until after the Farmer's Festival. Not if he wanted his father's blessing when he received his own land.

Juan turned and waved when he heard Rosa shout. He almost shouted back but stopped when he saw her grandfather behind her. After they had driven their herd behind his, they made their way over. Don Francisco held out his hand. "How are you this morning?" he asked.

Juan's hand tingled and felt warm. "I'm better," he said.

"And your mother?"

"She's fine," Juan said.

The old man's mouth tightened, but he didn't say anything else. He turned to Rosa, and she kissed him on the cheek. Her grandfather nodded and walked back toward the village.

Rosa took a few coca leaves from Juan and tucked them inside her cheek. They followed the herd through the rocky ford and up the switchbacks. The animals spread out around them when they reached the top, tearing at clumps of grass wedged between the rocks.

"I wonder why your grandfather is so concerned about my mother," Juan said. "Yesterday he asked me to offer his sympathies to her. This morning he's concerned about how she's doing."

Rosa laughed. "He sounds gruffer than he is. After you left, he asked a lot of questions about you and the jaguar. Especially when I shared…never mind about that," she said. "How is your mother really doing?"

"Worse than you can imagine," Juan said. "I haven't seen her so upset since…in a long time." He wasn't ready to talk about Marta with Rosa. Not yet. "So what did you tell your grandfather?" he asked.

"Only that you were very brave and that you probably saved my life."

"Why did you go and tell him that?" Juan was embarrassed, scared, and pleased. He pretended not to see Rosa look at him, but he saw a hint of a smile on her face. He picked up a pebble and bounced it off the back end of a burro that threatened to kick the calf.

"Because that jaguar could have killed us," Rosa said. "And you stood up and faced it. You did a brave thing, Juanito." She pulled on a cord that dangled beneath his hat. "I left the part out about how you pulled me down," she said.

He shot her a wry look. "I was trying to keep you from getting eaten," he said.

"My grandfather told me that what you did was an act of power. Anyone who takes a stand to protect another, he said, is a person of honor." Rosa prodded the calf away from the back feet of the burro with her stick.

"Don Francisco said that?" he said. She smiled and nodded. Her eyes looked different this morning. It was the way she

looked at him. He pointed to the rim of the plateau on the right.
"We need to move the herd. The grass is better over there," he
said. "And we'll still be able to keep the village in sight."

The morning sun slipped through a bank of clouds.
A moving shadow lengthened and shortened across the rolling
terrain in front of them. Juan shaded his face and looked up.
He pointed toward the condor that soared overhead.

"Hatun Kuntur," Rosa said. "It's the guide to the upper
world. You remember the story that Doña Mariana told us when
we were little?"

"I remember," he said. "Even then, her face showed more
wrinkles than skin. And when she opened her mouth, she had
barely enough teeth to hold that wad of coca leaves against her
cheek. She was ancient even when we were kids."

"Doña Mariana has learned a lot in her years," Rosa said.
"Do you remember what she said about the great condor that
flies between heaven and earth and sees through time? It flies
wingtip to wingtip with Spirit, she told us. And the wise learn
how to observe life from its point of view." Rosa chewed her coca
leaves thoughtfully and kept her eyes focused on the condor
that soared toward the mountains. The snow-capped peaks of
Ausangate, rarely free of clouds, were clear.

Juan worked his jaws around a weedy stem and watched dust
funnels drift across the ground in front of them. "My sister told
me that those are our ancestors dancing in the wind," he said.
"She said that they watched over us and would bring us back
home when we were lost."

"That's what my grandfather told me when I was little," Rosa
said.

"Marta told me that on the day that we came up here," Juan
said. "I would always pester her about going with her and the
herd. But she said that I was too little and that I would tire too
easily. I waited on the far side of the village one day and watched
for the cloud of dust from the herds coming home. When I saw
the red tassels of our lead llama, I took off running. Of course,
the animals scattered. That's when my sister promised that

I could go with her on my sixth birthday." He spit out the piece of grass. He was surprised by how easy it was to talk to Rosa about his sister.

"I loved her games," Rosa said. "Her stories turned San Mateo into a magical city. We were the rulers of the Incas, and all the people knew that we were from the Sun. Don't you remember?" Juan acted as if he didn't so that Rosa would continue. "My favorite times were when Marta became one of the ancestors, and we pretended that one of the hills that overlooked the village was Ausangate. Your sister said that she would give us the wisdom to lead our people, but we had to first climb the sacred mountain. Afterward, she told us that we would go there together someday. We would ask the ancient ones for their blessings so that we could be healers for the people of our *ayllu.*" Rosa pulled a handkerchief from her sleeve and blew her nose.

"I don't think much about those things anymore," Juan said. "Not since Marta…anyway, all that sounded different when I was little. Neither of us is a child anymore, that's for sure." He took the stem from his mouth and threw it on the ground.

Rosa cocked her head to one side and stared at him like he was a puzzle that she had yet to figure out. He shifted his seat and sat up. "Why do you look at me like that?" he said.

"You don't let your dreams go just because you grow up," she said. She stood and brushed the grass from her skirts. "Don't you remember how we begged my grandfather and Doña Mariana to teach us? We were only five, but we stood on that hill and made a promise to each other. Maybe that isn't important to you anymore, but it is to me." She tossed her braid over her shoulder and walked away. Juan's ears burned beneath the flaps of his wool cap. He had worked hard to put the past behind him. The dream that Rosa was talking about had died with Marta. In two days he would have land of his own to farm. That should be enough.

The sun slid out from a bank of cumulus clouds when Rosa sat back down beside him. She reached inside a pouch. "I thought you might like some lunch," she said. The corn tamale that she held out reminded him how hungry he was. Juan took it from her hand with a grateful nod. The bits of chicken wrapped in cornmeal disappeared in several bites. He sucked the last few morsels from his teeth and thought about what he wanted to say. Rosa's eyes had an expectant look when he looked at her.

"At night, after we crawled under the covers together and before our parents came to bed, Marta would tell me stories that she'd heard from your grandfather and Doña Mariana," Juan said. "She always started them with 'Once there was a little boy and his sister.' Her tales were about strange places, like hot springs that bubbled up from deep inside the earth. She said that the water would keep you warm even on the coldest of days."

"I like that one," Rosa said. Her chest brushed against his arm when she scooted closer. Juan could smell the mint-like *muña* on her breath. He tried not to think about her without any clothes on, sitting next to him in the hot water. She looked at him with that funny half-smile. Her eyebrows rose and tip of her tongue played along the rough edge of her front tooth.

"But before you could enter the water, you had to ask permission," he said.

Rosa's brown eyes widened. Juan blushed. He pretended that he didn't notice that her hand rested on his shoulder. "With Marta, every story was about spiritual things," he said. "You had to ask Sachamama, a serpent who was the guardian spirit. Only those who were worthy could enter into her world."

"Were you scared?"

"Maybe. But my sister could make anything sound like a big adventure," Juan said.

"What else did she say?"

"Marta said that Sachamama showed us how to shed our skin and become new again. She said we had to do this before we could help others. I told her that I would never shed my skin." Rosa laughed and squeezed his arm. His voice trembled with more excitement than he intended. "My sister said that this was how we healed our past. It was *ayni,* she said. When we release what we don't need, we get what we want. All real healers knew this, she said."

"My grandfather taught me this too. What we give is what we receive," Rosa said. "*Ayni* keeps us in harmony with Mother Earth. It brings us into balance with who we are. When we forget that, we get ourselves into trouble, he said."

"Marta talked a lot with your grandfather."

Rosa sighed. "I miss her," she said.

Juan scanned the horizon. With the passing clouds gone, the rays of the afternoon sun connected the edges of the yellow pastures with a web of spun light. Gusts of wind rippled through the coarse grass. The animals grazed beneath the ridge. Juan looked at Rosa. "Take a walk with me," he said. "We'll stay close to the herd."

He stood, grabbed her wrist, and pulled her up. She tugged at the bottom of her sweater, stretching the alpaca weave across her wide shoulders and over her chest. She swept off her backside, adjusted the layered skirt around her waist, and tucked some loose strands of hair behind her ear. The thick fingers and broken nails spoke of weaving and working in her mother's garden. Rosa smiled when she caught his eyes and slipped her hand inside his. Juan shouted at one of the burros at the bottom of the hill.

Chapter Six

They hiked along the crest, keeping the village to the west and the mountain to the east. The condor, lifted by the thermal currents over the peaks of Ausangate, was barely visible. They watched until it disappeared. "Did you ever wonder how small San Mateo would look if you were standing on top of that mountain?" Rosa said.

It sounded like a question that his sister would ask. Anything was possible in her magical world. Marta's games always started out with "Let's play like…" She told him that he could travel anywhere if he could just imagine it. "Sometimes when I see an eagle, I pretend that it's me and then everything looks small," Juan said. "But I don't get much time to think about those things. My father gets upset when he catches me daydreaming like that. He says that I should keep my mind on farming. Maybe he's right."

"My grandfather has farmed for most of his life," Rosa said. "And he's been healing people since before my mother was born. When I talked with him last night, he said that what happened with that jaguar was no accident. It was a message."

A knot lodged inside Juan's chest. "About what?" he asked.

"I asked him, but he never answers my questions directly," Rosa said. "He said that every person has to face Otorongo someday. The spirit of the jaguar stalks us from the day we are born and it finds us on the day of our death. Life happens in between these two times, my grandfather said. He told me that the jaguar is a great teacher. Those that look into its eyes without fear can create their own destiny. That's the path the shaman walks, he said."

Juan wasn't sure what Rosa meant. When he had looked into that jaguar's eyes yesterday, he was scared. He knew that it could kill him, but he stood up and faced it. But it was different when he thought about the day that Marta died. That fear haunted his dreams, and he was powerless to stop it. He felt Rosa's hand slip from his arm and looked back. She stood with a crooked pout on her lips.

"I'm listening," he said. "What else did your grandfather say?"

"He told me that the jaguar had come for you, but you were the only one who could decide whether to follow its tracks. If you want to know anything more, you'll have to talk to my grandfather," she said. She put her hand back on his arm. He knew where this was going. First it was his parents and now her. Everyone, it seemed, knew what was best for him.

Rosa squeezed his arm. "Don't be upset with me," she said. "You can still farm. I just thought that…when you were a boy, you were always trying to help things get better. Remember when Pepe and you found that baby gopher? You took it home, and you tried to keep it alive by blowing into its mouth?"

He saw the bull calf drop its nose against the ground behind one of the burros. The burro had its ears laid back, twitching its tail from side to side. Juan ran down the hillside shouting when the burro arched its back and dropped its head. The cow's iron bell clanged when she charged in to protect the bawling calf. The rest of the herd trotted a safe distance away. With his hands on his knees, he watched the cow lick her calf. "Great," he muttered.

"What's wrong?" Rosa asked.

"That calf's hurt," he said. "It's limping on the right front leg. That stupid burro must have connected with it pretty good." He got his hand on the rope around the cow's neck and worked his way back to the calf until he could slide his arm behind its head. "Hold him like this," he told Rosa. The calf's eyes flashed white when she held the head against her shoulder. She talked to it with a voice that one might use to soothe a frightened child. The cow sniffed Rosa's head with moist snorts.

The calf struggled when Juan touched its knee. Only the tip of its hoof touched the ground when he began to run his hands along its leg. Nothing was broken, but already the joint was hot and swollen. He let his hands nestle around the knee and began to breathe in rhythm with the calf. It was what his mother had taught him. Just let your hands do the work, she said. He closed his eyes and imagined that his breath came from his navel.

His hands grew warm and a tingly sensation moved up his arms. The swelling underneath his fingers softened, and he could feel the bone. The calf bawled in Rosa's ear. She laughed when the cow started to lick the top of her head. By the time he stood up, the calf's foot rested flat against the ground. It turned around and thrust its nose against the cow's udder.

"You have a way with animals like your mother," Rosa said. "I've watched you with the herd. Just like with that burro. You could tell what it was going to do before it ever moved."

"I'd rather be with animals," Juan said. "I like to work with them. When I stand a newborn alpaca or calf on its wobbly legs and hold its mouth to its mother's teats, I feel that I've done something."

"Couldn't you be a healer for people too?" Rosa asked. Her eyes were sleepy-like when she looked at him.

Juan worked the muscles in his jaw. "What if a person came to me and they died?" he said. "What if someone else could have saved them?" But he knew that it was more than that. And he saw that Rosa knew it too.

"You've never told me what happened," she said. "Marta was my best friend."

The lull in the wind deepened the silence on top of the ridge. He rubbed his face hard. He had forgotten how tired he got when he thought about that day. When he was a boy, his mother told him that bad memories grew old and died, but that the good ones lived forever. After the nightmares stopped, he figured that they had gone for good. They had until his sister, riding on the back of a jaguar, chased him in his dream the other morning.

"There is not a day that goes by that I don't think about Marta and that day of the storm," he said. "Our father warned that the dark clouds around Ausangate could turn into a nasty storm. It would be best for my sister to go by herself and keep the herd close to the village, he said. Even she tried to convince me to stay home. I could go another time, she said."

"Why did you go?" Rosa asked.

"Marta was more like an older brother than a sister. I even tried to walk like her. Ever since I was five, she had promised we would take the herd together on my birthday. I was six years old, and it was my birthday."

"And your father didn't stop you?"

"I told him that I would just walk to the edge of the village with Marta. Instead, I talked her into taking me to the high pasture. I told her that she had given me her word. She shouldn't let a few stupid clouds spoil my birthday, I said."

"And you blame yourself for what happened," Rosa said.

"It was more than that. She had gone to talk with your grandfather several weeks before. When she came back, she had a faraway look in her eyes. But my sister wouldn't tell me what it was about. I was mad at her. She had always shared everything with me. When we drove the herd up to the grasslands, I ran behind the animals and hurried them up the trail. Marta lagged behind. She seemed lost. I walked back to talk with her, but I don't think she even knew I was there. Something was wrong. I wish that I would have told her to take me home then."

His mouth was dry and pasty. He closed his eyes, took a deep breath, and swallowed. He could see the lightning flicker inside the black clouds and hear the thunder that rumbled in the distance. When the wind-whipped dust pelted him and his sister, the animals had stamped their feet and milled around in circles.

"What happened?" asked Rosa.

"The sky turned blacker than night before we knew what hit us," he said. "I got scared and wanted to run toward the village, but Marta grabbed me. She said that it was too late to go back. We had to find shelter until the storm blew over. There was a cave nearby that she'd found several weeks ago. We would be safe there, she told me."

"But what happened then?" Rosa asked.

A sick feeling stirred at the bottom of Juan's stomach. "We didn't make it to the cave," he said. "The next time I opened my eyes was when I heard my father shout my name. He carried me down to the village while others rounded up the herd. It was the only time that I've ever seen him cry. They brought my sister down wrapped inside a blanket. For a long time afterward, my mother would cry and hug me whenever she looked at me. But my father never talked to me much after that. I hear him mention Marta's name sometimes when he thinks that he and my mother are alone. He still blames me for what happened."

Rosa wiped her face with the back of her hand. The muted light of the westerly sun sat heavy on her face. "My heart was broken the day they brought back Marta's body," she said, "but when I came to tell you how sorry I was you wouldn't even talk to me. My grandfather said to give you more time. But you didn't want to be my friend anymore."

"I was afraid that you blamed me for Marta's death too," Juan said.

Rosa's hand was gentle when she touched his face. "My heart aches for Marta," she said. "She was my sister too. But never have I blamed you for her death."

He could only look into Rosa's eyes for a moment. But it was enough. He nodded.

"My grandfather says that regret ties us to our past," she said. "It's best to let it go and to move on."

Juan shrugged his shoulders and sighed. "I suppose he's right," he said.

Rosa's eyes crinkled. "And you still avoid me," she said. "Even when I try to talk with you, all you do is to mumble and walk away."

He pulled off his hat, scratched his head, and pretended to study his fingernails. "Every guy in San Mateo tries to catch your eye these days," he said. "I don't like being around when you flirt with them."

Juan winced when she dug her elbow into his side. "I talk to lots of people, including boys, if it suits me," she said. "If you come around more, maybe I'll flirt with you." Rosa laughed and nudged him again. "Promise you'll talk with my grandfather."

"When he hit my chest yesterday, I saw that jaguar again," he said. She covered her mouth. "It's not funny," he grumbled. He wasn't ready to tell her about seeing through the jaguar's eyes.

"You can talk to him about that too," she said. Juan shot her a suspicious look. He wondered how much she knew.

"Let it go for now," he said. "Maybe that jaguar came up from the jungle looking for a quick meal, and it's gone back already." He knew that neither one of them believed that, but he didn't want to talk about it anymore. Every time he thought about that jaguar, it gave him a headache.

"My grandfather says that jaguar came for you."

Juan wondered if the shaman knew about the nightmare that woke him up the other morning. "I heard the whispers and felt the stares when I walked through the village yesterday. But that's nothing new. Ever since that day of the storm, people have thought I must have been born under the wrong star. This thing with the jaguar will only make it worse. They'll talk about me just like they do about my mother," he said. "The other women of the village come to her for readings when their husbands are gone, but they shake their heads when they hear her talk to the animals in that voice of hers. And they say things behind her back, clucking their tongues about how hard it must be for us children to have a mother who's deaf." Rosa opened her mouth, but Juan raised his hand.

"The other day, my little sisters came home crying because the other kids made fun of my mother. They still tell that old story about when I was a baby and she would work in her garden. They hear it from their mothers. They said that a mountain lion came and lay on that rise in back of our house every day. It showed up after the men left to go work in the fields and was gone when they returned. My mother would talk to it like it was a long lost friend."

"I remember hearing that story when I was a little girl," Rosa said.

"And when my father found out, he became filled with rage and drove the mountain lion away. It never returned and it was never mentioned by either of them again."

"But you shouldn't let what others say bother you," she said. "Don't you know how special your mother is? My grandfather says she sees more in people's faces than they can in a mirror."

"It is one thing to be respected like your grandfather. But I don't want to be made fun of and I don't want to be pitied."

"Our *allyu* isn't like that. The people here respect your mother," Rosa said. "It's important that you talk with my grandfather. He said when a jaguar shows up, a wise person pays attention. He has more to say, but it's up to you to go visit him."

Juan watched the light deepen inside the clouds around the mountain. He knew that if he talked with Don Francisco, the old man would see that his sister's ghost still haunted him.

"Maybe I'm better off just being a farmer like my father," he said.

Rosa threw her hands up in the air. "You are so stubborn," she said. "Why can't you just go and talk with him?" She stood with her hands on her hips.

Her eyes showed no sign of budging. He held out his hand. "I'll think about it," he said. "But for now, we need to take the herd back down."

Rosa shook her head. "You were my best friend when we were little," she said. "I've always believed that it would be that way again. I know how hard it's been for you since Marta died. But I have to know what your dream is. It's important to me. Can you understand?"

He dug his toes into the dark, weathered leather of his sandals. The nagging wind that swirled gritty dust around his feet tugged at the hair over his eyes. He dropped his hand. It was clear that Rosa wasn't going to be happy until he talked to her grandfather.

It would be more than just a visit if he talked to the shaman. That jaguar was after him because of Marta. He was sure of it.

Chapter Seven

He chased the herd from behind. The remnants of daylight disappeared behind dark clouds filled with unrelenting rain. He turned when his sister shouted at him. She rode a black jaguar. Dark tresses hung over her shoulders, blending in with the beast's fur. Her bare legs were pressed behind its massive shoulders. Lightning flashed, covering her with a shroud of blue light. Her face was charred. Blood trickled from the corner of her mouth. "Run, Juanito, run," she screamed. A clap of thunder exploded behind him. But his feet were stuck in deep black clay. The jaguar roared and leapt toward him. His sister stretched out her hand to grab him. Juan yelled at the top of his voice, but only a faint moan came from his throat.

"Juanito, wake up, my son, you're having another bad dream," his mother said. She shook his shoulder. "You're waking the other children. Get up and come help me," she whispered. It was his mother who had comforted him when he was little. She would rock him and hum a tuneless sound when he awakened crying and kicking his legs. If only he could stay close to her, then he would be safe from the bad dreams, he had thought.

He crawled out from underneath the covers, rubbing his eyes. He broke up a couple of eucalyptus branches and wedged them into the oven until it crackled with fire. When he grabbed the kettle off the hearth, he was surprised that it was already heavy.

"Your father filled it," his mother said. "He left early this morning with some of the men to go to Paucartambo for supplies. They'll be back late tonight." She set out two cups, took the kettle from Juan, and hung it over the fire. "Let's have some tea before the rest of the children wake up," she said. "It's been a while since we've talked, Juanito."

He moved around the open adobe oven, trying to avoid the smoke. His mother dropped a handful of coca leaves into the

43

kettle. They waited for the water to come to a boil. His mother fidgeted with her apron, trying to smooth out the wrinkles. Broken fingernails, stained dark with soot, slid back and forth over her lap.

"What it is?" Juan asked.

Her shoulders sagged. "It's hard for me to realize that tomorrow you will be eighteen. It was only a short time ago that you and Rosita were running through the village, chasing each other and playing games with your…you know…with all the other children."

"It's okay to say her name," he said. "It was Marta who played with us when we were little."

"Yes, of course, Juanito. I don't mean to upset you. You've been through so much," she said. "It's just that I thought that those dreams were behind you. It's been so long. I thought that…never mind. Things will be better now that you and Rosa are together again. You'll see," she said.

He stared into the fire, wishing that his mother would talk about Don Francisco's reading of the leaves. The nightmares were getting worse, not better. The steam rising from the kettle caught his eye. Before he could reach it, Wilhelmita picked up the handle with the edge of her apron. She filled one of the cups to the brim and handed it to him.

"Don't be angry with your mother. I only want you to be happy. The past few days have been hard on you, with that jaguar, and we have things that we need to talk about. But first drink your tea and tell me how you and Rosita are doing. Have you asked her to the dance yet?"

Juan flashed his mother a dark look. She didn't understand anything. She wasn't haunted by Marta, and that jaguar wasn't stalking her. The tea burned his lips, and he spit it out onto his poncho.

"Careful, you're spilling it on yourself," his mother said. She started to wipe his face with her apron, but he stepped back, rubbing the back of his hand against his chin.

"I don't need you to clean my face for me," Juan said. He shaped his words with emphasis. "Why do you always try to make me feel like a little boy? I don't need you to feel sorry for me.

I know that Marta's death was my fault. And I don't need your questions about Rosa, okay? Just leave me alone."

His mother's slap sounded like the snap of a branch. The cup fell from his hand. The hot water stung his feet, but he didn't move. He felt the imprint of his mother's anger against his cheek even more.

"Don't you ever talk to me like that again. I am still your mother, and you will respect me." Her high-pitched voice cracked, and her words rasped against the back of her throat. The raw edge to her voice left him ashamed. Her hands hung by her sides and her shoulders sagged. The children stirred under the covers. Juan walked over to the far side of the room in a daze.

"It's alright," he said. "Go back to sleep." He tucked the blankets around the restless bodies of his sisters. His brother mumbled and rolled over. Juan went back to the fire and watched the wood burn down into dark red embers. He flinched when he felt his mother's rough hand against his cheek. When he looked into her eyes, he saw the hurt. Rimmed in red, they searched his face for understanding.

"Don't be angry with your mother," she said. She patted the bench by the fire. "Let's talk, just you and me. Please." Wilhelmita refilled his cup and handed it to him. Juan sat so that she could see his lips.

"I'm sorry that I spoke to you like that," he said.

She shook her head and took his hand between hers. The corners of her mouth drooped and vertical wrinkles lined her upper lip. "Don't worry about me," she said. "Things have been hard for all of us lately. And I know that day of the storm was a terrible time for you, but it was hard on me and your father too. Not only did I lose my Marta that day, but my little boy, who laughed and who was so full of himself, left me also." His mother stared into the fire. "I should have known better," she said. "I should have insisted that both of you stay home on that day of the storm. If we had lost you too…"

His mother squeezed his hand against her chest. "I'm sorry for the pain that you've carried about Marta, but it wasn't your fault," she said. "Don Francisco said to see your sister die was a terrible shock for you. He told me we were lucky that you couldn't remember what happened during that storm. But it breaks my heart that the bad dreams still come to you. If I could make them stop, I would. All I have ever wanted is for you to be happy again."

Juan dug his nails into his palms. It was hard to look into his mother's eyes. He felt like he was still a little boy, searching her face for reassurance. Wilhelmita cupped her hand behind his neck and pulled his head against her wool sweater. The smell of smoke, garlic, and sweat flooded into him. His mother rubbed his back, rocking him back and forth, humming a tuneless song. "Everything will be okay," she said.

Chapter Eight

"Your brother is well enough to take care of the herd, Juanito. Come help me in the garden today," his mother said. José grinned and slapped him on the shoulder on his way out the door. Wilhelmita shouted at him not to forget his lunch. When she finished dressing Maria and Anna, she sent them out to pick *muña*. The weedy plant with a mint-like taste would make a good tea for Papá's stomach, she told them. She shoved a handful of potatoes beside the coals and threw several cups of quinoa grain into a pot of water and covered it with a lid. Juan followed her outside into the garden behind the house.

His mother lifted the long wooden hoe and dropped the heavy head into the brown clay with a practiced swing. Even as a young girl, she had worked alongside the men in the fields, providing for her and her mother. When he first started to help her in the garden, she had showed him how to use the hoe the right way. "Don't just hit the ground," she said, "but grab it and swing it up high. Let the weight at the end of your hoe do the work. There is nothing better than to work with the earth and know that she will give you something good to eat."

He followed Wilhelmita from one row to the next. He pulled the weeds that grew too close to the stalks for a hoe to cut. Before he took over the herd, he had been her helper. He was her ears when the women of the *ayllu* met. He told her what they said when she could not see their lips. And he negotiated for her when the traders from Paucartambo came to San Mateo and bought the blankets, sweaters, and the cloth that the women wove.

Juan told the traders that she was deaf, not hard of hearing. Still, they would shout their words within inches of her face. It distorted their lips so much that she could not understand them. And she hated that they spit in her face when they talked. It was

47

easier if Juan spoke for her. But sometimes it could be awkward. His mother ordered him to tell one man, who wanted to give her far less than what her blankets were worth, that he was a big idiot and that she would never sell him anything. When she read Juan's lips, she caught him telling the trader that she would think about his offer. She gripped his shoulder and fixed him with a fierce stare. "You speak my words, not your words," his mother told him.

Many in the village said that she had learned to read more than just lips. When he was little, Juan would sit beside her when other women came to her for private readings, sharing things they could confide only to another woman. His mother taught him to read their faces, how to tell when the eyes contradicted what their lips were saying.

When they worked together in the garden, she would tell Juan stories about her childhood. He would ask her questions, knowing which ones would bring forth his favorites. Whenever he asked about her parents, Wilhelmita would lower her voice to a whisper. She was born out of wedlock, she said, the only child of a young woman forced to marry an older man after the family of her lover had forbidden their marriage. Her stepfather had been cruel to her and her mother. He reminded them of how he had taken them in when no one else would. He would disappear for days at a time, leaving her to fend for herself and for a mother who was ill much of the time.

She worked in the fields when the other children played with their friends. Rather than crushing her, she told her son, it made her determined to work harder than any of the men. She got to where she could hoe faster than anyone. One day a man came up to her because he could not catch his new burro. She walked up to the animal and slipped the rope halter over his head like it belonged to her. His mother told Juan that its owner became her closest friend after that.

He watched her chop weeds several rows over. Finally he walked over and touched her shoulder before she lifted the hoe again. Startled, his mother stopped and faced him. Juan moved his lips carefully. "You've known Rosa's grandfather for a long time, haven't you?"

She leaned on her hoe and wiped her brow with her sleeve. Her flustered look surprised him. "Of course, I know Francisco José. Everyone in the village knows him. Why do you ask?"

"Remember when you were a young girl, and that man asked you to catch his new burro for him?"

"I remember," Wilhelmita said.

"That was Don Francisco, wasn't it?"

She gazed at the hillside overlooking the garden. "He had quite a temper in those days and struggled with his anger," she said. "I think that how I caught his burro made an impression. At first, he barely acknowledged what I had done. He took the rope from my hand and mumbled thanks before he turned and walked away. The next morning I found a bundle of corn tamales outside our door. Your grandmother and I certainly appreciated them," she said.

"Others were afraid of him, but he was kind to me. He told me his name was Francisco José. And that is what I've always called him." She looked around before she spoke again. "Over time, he began to talk with me. I found out that his father had left when he was young, leaving him to care for his mother and his sister. Like me, he had to be too old too soon. He barely knew what it was to be a boy before he became a man. He was the only one besides my mother with whom I could share my feelings. He saw how much pain I carried inside. We became friends and talked often in the fields when we worked together," she said.

"You were friends with Don Francisco?" said Juan.

"What a sight we must have made," she said. Wilhelmita held her hand over her mouth and laughed. "The feared shaman and a struggling girl, too young to be afraid, swinging their hoes side by side. But I tell you this. He watched over me and my mother, helping us when my stepfather wasn't around. Over time, he taught me how to see beneath the words that people spoke. He said that I was already good at reading faces. And he saw that I had a gift."

"What kind of gift?" Juan said.

His mother's eyes lit up. "Francisco José had a fine herd of alpacas and llamas. Early one morning, he rescued a newborn llama from a mother that had twins and wouldn't let this one nurse. He didn't think that it would live, but he said that I could have her if I wanted. He let me milk his cow and gave me a bottle for the baby llama to suckle. She stayed with me at night, curled in my arms, and we fell asleep together."

"Was that La Reina's mother, Francesca?" he asked.

His mother nodded. "She followed me everywhere, grazing along the edges of the fields where we worked during the day. She was the most beautiful creature that I had ever seen. I combed her shiny black coat until she sparkled, and I wove strands of red yarn along her neck and onto her ears."

Wilhelmita shook her head. "But enough of these stories," she said. "There's work to be done." She put her hand on his shoulder and lowered her voice. "This is just between you and me. Never discuss any of this with your father."

"Why does he hate him?" Juan asked. "What did Rosa's grandfather ever do to him?"

His mother rubbed the back of her hand against her mouth. She looked past him toward the end of the row. Tiny swirls of dust moved through the village streets. "They had a falling out long before you were born. Your father was like a son to Francisco José. But Humberto's never going to change his mind about him. It doesn't matter now. I've got to finish my rows. That woman is coming to talk with me this afternoon."

There was something else he had to ask her. Yesterday he wouldn't have imagined that it was possible. Now he wasn't sure. "That mountain lion who came to visit you in the garden was more than just a mountain lion, wasn't it?"

He saw the hurt in his mother's eyes before she took the hoe back into her hands. She swung the metal head in a high arc before she drove it into the ground. The corn stalks shook and the leaves rattled against one another. She swung the hoe in a thudding rhythm up one row and down the next. Her eyes remained fixed on the ground ahead. Juan realized that his mother's world had narrowed to a piece of earth that no longer included him.

Chapter Nine

He sat back on his heels between the rows of corn and watched Wilhelmita work through the rest of the garden. Wiping the sweat from her brow with her sleeve was the only thing that interrupted the steady swing of her hoe. He knew his mother, and she was not going to answer any more questions, at least not about a mountain lion. She jumped when Juan touched her shoulder from behind. She leaned on her hoe and waited for him to step around.

Juan saw that it wasn't anger but sadness that dulled her eyes.

"What do you want?" she said.

"Rosa thinks that I should talk with Don Francisco," Juan said. He was going to wait until after the festival, but with his father gone, there would never be a better time. He followed his mother's gaze through the stalks of corn and out across the fields to the mountains east of the village. Her eyebrows rose like wings across her forehead, and the vertical lines in her lips softened. It was that look that came over her face that always transformed her stories into visions that she saw in the moment of the telling. Even when he was little, he would put all of his attention on her lips and pretend to be deaf. That way he could slip into her world unnoticed and see everything that she described. Juan watched his mother speak.

"Your father wanted a son, and we asked Doña Mariana to prepare a *despacho* for us," she said. "Her gift to Mother Earth took a long time to prepare. After we left, she burned the *despacho* over her fire. I knew that she read the flames like Don Francisco reads the leaves. When I saw her later, I asked her to tell me what she saw. She said that we would have a son and that the jaguar spirit would be strong in him. After you were born, we celebrated your baptism at the Farmer's Festival. I wanted

51

to take you to Francisco José, but I knew that your father would forbid it."

"But why?" he asked.

"He had his reasons," she said. "But in my heart I knew that you had a destiny that stretched beyond his vision for you. I prayed that you would be a healer like Don Francisco. After you were baptized, I wanted to hear what he would say. He's the most respected *kurak akullek* of the Andes. Such a person who 'chews the leaves' can see into the future. So I waited until your father was drinking *chicha*, celebrating with his friends. The buckets were full with corn beer, and Humberto was in no rush to go. When I told him that I was leaving, he thought that I was tired and wanted to go home. But I took you to Francisco José's house.

"He was surprised to see me at his door. It had been years since I'd been there. At first, he didn't want to do it. But when I persisted, he finally agreed to read the leaves for me. He grabbed several handfuls of coca leaves from his bag and spread them out over his medicine cloth. He picked through them until he held three sets of three leaves between each of his fingers. He blew on them and chanted words that I couldn't understand, and then he threw them down onto his *mesa*. They landed in different lines on the cloth, some bunched together and some spread apart. He pointed out the tiniest of details, noting when one leaf leaned against the other and when one stuck out from the rest. When he stared at you, it was like he was looking into another world."

"But what did he say," Juan asked.

"'Bring him to me,' he said. He cut off a piece of your hair with a black obsidian knife and laid it on the cloth. He took you from my hands and held you up against the light of the fire. When you reached for his little finger, his face filled with such a look of wonder. That's when he saw the scar in the middle of your left hand." His mother turned Juan's palm upward and traced the scar beneath his ring finger.

"But what else did he say?"

Wilhelmita let go of his hand. The wrinkles on her brow deepened, and her voice wavered when she spoke. "He started to say something, but he didn't. There was anguish in his eyes. Francisco José saw more than he wanted to see. He told me not to let you go with Marta to the high pastures until your seventh birthday. After that day of the storm, I knew what he had seen in the leaves." Her lips quivered and she wiped her eyes with her apron.

"He said that scar in your hand was the mark of the great condor and that you would have the gift of seeing through the eyes of Hatun Kuntur, if you chose," Wilhelmita said. "But you had to choose wisely. He said that such vision came with a great price, and it could be dangerous."

"Dangerous?"

"He warned that the gift of seeing into the upper world could be intoxicating, much more than any amount of *chicha* that one might drink. If such sight became disconnected from the heart, it would be a relentless master, driving a person in ways that caused pain for them and for others," said his mother.

"I've heard Papá talk about those who walk the streets of Paucartambo and utter strange incantations," Juan said. "And he's told me about *los brujos,* the sorcerers who work with dark magic."

"For sure, but let's not speak of such things," Wilhelmita said. "Francisco José held out a much higher vision for your destiny. He said that there would be much to learn before you could walk the path of the jaguar. The call to be a shaman came with great challenges. You would need to go deeper before you could go higher, he said."

"What did he mean?"

"He said that you would have to harvest your own corn before you could help others. You would have to follow the jaguar's tracks to where the ancient ones live. 'He must learn to create his own destiny,' he said. This is how he described the path of the shaman." Wilhelmita sighed and eased herself down onto a flat rock by the side of the garden.

"What did he tell you about the jaguar?" Juan said.

His mother looked away. "It's best that you ask him about such things. He said that to become a shaman was much more of an inside journey than a physical one. When you knew who you were, you could see from a higher place and summon your destiny, he told me."

Juan rubbed his hand. He glanced at his mother. She was staring at his scar. "Why didn't you tell me about this before?" he asked.

She shrugged her shoulders. "It's been hard for me not to talk about it with you. So many times I've wanted to tell you, but he made me promise not to."

"Don Francisco didn't want you to tell me?" Juan said. "I thought it was Papá."

"You don't understand," his mother said. "Francisco José said that I had to wait until the time was right. When Otorongo came, then it would be for you to choose your path. I know now that what happened with La Reina was no accident." His mother put her hand on his shoulder. "The death of the llama was a sign. That jaguar came for you."

A shiver ran through Juan. It was worse than he had expected. His mother had been in on this from the beginning with Don Francisco. This thing about the jaguar wasn't going away. But what would happen when the shaman found out that he wasn't worthy to follow this path?

He wanted to ask his mother, but she put her hand up. "It is not for me to say what you should do," she said. "It is for you to decide."

A flash of green and violet buzzed Juan's head. He tried to see where the bird went, but it had already disappeared.

"Juanito, did you see that?" his mother said.

"It was a hummingbird," he said. "But that kind is from the jungle. It's strange to see one here."

Wilhelmita nodded. "Odd indeed," she said.

All he needed was another creature to stalk him. It was time to do what had to be done. His mother's eyes fixed on his lips. "Maybe now is a good time for me to talk with Rosa's grandfather," he said. "The neighbor's boy was taking the herd up to the pastures today, and I think that Don Francisco is home," he stammered. "That is, if you can get by without me for a while."

The corners of his mother's eyes crinkled. "I think that Rosa will be home too." She handed him a straw basket. "Pick some ears of corn, and I'll be back in a moment." After he broke off a dozen ears of corn, he placed them inside the basket with the silky tassels on top. She came back with several small bags. "I filled these with tobacco and coca leaves," she said. She laid them on top of the corn and added, "Tell Francisco José that I hope he is well." Her eyes had that faraway look again.

Juan gave her a quick hug and stepped out onto the dirt path. Her singsong voice warbled behind him. "Don't forget to ask Rosita to the dance," she cried out. "It's tomorrow, you know."

He cringed, but he pretended not to hear. Several women who were passing by stopped and smiled at him.

Chapter Ten

Juan stiffened his chest and made his voice sound deeper. "Don Francisco, I am here to talk about the day that you read the leaves for my mother." He imagined saying the words to the shaman's face and said them louder. His ears grew warm when he saw a woman in an open doorway, holding a baby in her arms. A toddler peeked out from behind her skirts.

A group of village women sat on the ground and wove different colored strands of alpaca wool into cloth. At one end the strands were tied to their waists and at the other to sticks braced against their feet. Their hands moved with a steady rhythm, keeping the fabric taut with shuttles made from pieces of wood and llama bone. Juan felt their eyes follow him down the street. Little girls laughed and stirred cast iron pots filled with dyes and heated over smoldering fires. Older girls, spinning the yarn around bobbing spindles, flashed smiles at him. He was a one-person parade walking through the village of San Mateo. He stared at the basket of corn in front of him.

When he rounded the corner toward Rosa's house, he almost bumped into the old woman who stepped out from a side door. The elfin woman steadied herself on a crooked wooden stick and chuckled. A wide grin covered the deeply wrinkled face. Her vest, bright crimson embroidered with gold thread, was buttoned across a sagging chest that rested on her belly. Two white braids hung on either side. Doña Mariana peered up at him with diverging eyes, tinted with the blue of time. Juan looked from one eye to the other before he decided which one to follow.

"Where are you going in such a rush this morning, young man?" she asked. She took a pinch of coca leaves from a bag that hung from her side and tucked them into her cheek pouch.

"I'm sorry. I didn't see you, Doña Mariana," Juan said. "I'm running an errand for my mother."

She nodded, the back of her short-brimmed white straw hat brushing against the padded hump behind her neck. "Those are pretty ears of corn in your basket. Your mother always has a good garden." He shifted the basket to one side and glanced toward Rosa's house. An old black dog with a gray muzzle lay asleep in front. "I think that she went with the rest of the family to Paucartambo this morning. Today is market day there," the old woman said.

"Oh? Yes, of course," he said.

She fixed Juan with an odd stare. One eye peered keenly into his face and the other looked to the side. "She's such a lovely girl," she said. "And she is so devoted to her grandfather. Even when she was a little girl, she slept in his house more than her own. Of course, he's very protective of his Rosita. That's why most boys wait to talk with her when he's not around," Doña Mariana laughed.

A morning breeze stirred through the village. Broken clouds dotted the dark blue sky, creating odd-shaped shadows on the ground that Juan followed with his eyes. He shoved his bangs underneath his hat and shrugged. "Maybe I will come back another time."

The old woman shuffled closer and laid a thin, bony hand against his chest. She peered into his face. Tilting her head to one side, she stared at him as though he were a newborn. Her mouth opened, showing the few dark teeth that held a green wad of leaves against her cheek. "It's important that you talk with her grandfather," she said. "It is a good day to visit him. Go on. He's home now. The tobacco and coca leaves that Wilhelmita sent will mean the world to him."

Juan hesitated, unsure of what had changed her tone. He reached into the basket, grabbed a couple of ears of corn, and offered them to her. "Please take these," he said.

She took the ears and held them against her chest. "Bless you and your mother. Of course, I have to cut the kernels off the cob these days," she laughed. "You go on. Don Francisco's waiting for you. And don't worry. His bark is worse than his bite. If he likes you, that is." She grinned and wiped her mouth with the

back of her hand. He stepped aside to let her pass. She tapped
her stick against the ground in front of her and disappeared
around the corner.

The old dog in front of Rosa's house opened an eye when
Juan walked past and stretched out his limbs before he resumed
his nap. Secluded in a grove of eucalyptus trees, Don Francisco's
house sat at the far end of the street. Poles sat stacked to one
side of the empty stone corral. The heavy wood door was partly
opened, sagging on worn hinges. Juan took a deep breath. His
hand paused in midair when Don Francisco's voice rumbled
from inside. "Come in and shut the door behind you," he said.

Juan ducked underneath the low doorway and stepped into
the smoke-filled room. Don Francisco stood with his back to the
fire. Claws that could have only come from a jaguar hung from
a leather cord around his neck. Juan swallowed, but his throat
stayed dry in the smoky air. "The corn is from my mother," he
said. He wiped one palm against his poncho, reached into the
basket, and picked up the two bags. "She sent these too."

The old man nodded shyly and took them. He pointed
across the room. "Put that basket over there, if you can find
a place for it," he said. He pursed his lips to push his breath
out. Rosa had told Juan that was why her grandfather's chest
was so barrel-shaped. He had a hard time getting air out of his
lungs. Her mother had threatened to take him to the doctor in
Paucartambo, but one look from her grandfather put a stop to
that idea, she said.

Juan stepped around a large rawhide drum, careful not to hit
his head on the pots and pans that hung down from the wooden
rafters. Different piles of plants and herbs lay piled in bunches
on the part of the packed-dirt floor uncovered by rugs. Pieces
of San Pedro cactus leaned against the stone walls. The familiar
smell of *muña* filled the room. It made a good tea for digestion
and for mental alertness, he thought. He could use a cup now.

He studied the weavings that covered the walls. A yellow
snake lay coiled on a gray tapestry. Two condors flew wingtip to
wingtip across a blue background. But it was the black jaguar
with piercing yellow eyes that held his attention. A green

hummingbird trimmed in purple hung above its head on the dark red cloth. It was the mythic jaguar, Otorongo, with Q'inti hovering over its head. His father had told him that the sighting of this hummingbird in the jungle often foretold the appearance of a jaguar. It was the other way around in his experience, Juan thought. He turned around when he heard the old man's cough.

Don Francisco raised his eyebrows. "How is your mother," he said.

"She is much better."

"And the rest of the family?"

"They are well," Juan said.

Steam spit from the kettle behind the shaman. Sticks of green eucalyptus wood burned hot inside the adobe oven, popping with an occasional burst of sparks.

Juan sat the basket down and cleared his throat. "I came to talk with you."

Don Francisco gestured with his head toward the fire. "Grab some cups off the shelf there," he said. The shaman's hands shook when he picked up the kettle, spilling the coca tea when he poured. Juan held the cups steady and pretended not to notice the drops when they spattered on his skin. The old man dragged a couple of straw mats into the middle of the room. "Bring the tea and come sit down," he said.

The craggy face, softened by the dim light, reminded Juan of childhood stories about the ancestors who had come from Lago Titicaca to found Cusco, the center of the Inca Empire. Manco Capac showed the men how to farm, and Mamá Ocllo taught the women to weave. He remembered when he was little that he thought that Don Francisco must have known them.

The shaman's eyes brightened when Juan handed him a cup and sat down across from him. "So what is it that you want to talk about?" he asked.

He wondered how long the old man had been waiting for him. Maybe he had always known that he would come someday. "I want to know about the day you read the leaves for my mother," he said.

Don Francisco lifted his shaggy white eyebrows, pursed his lips, and took a sip of tea. He stared thoughtfully at the door.

Juan wasn't sure what else to say. Maybe he'd spoken too loud inside the small house. He tried hard not to let his doubts show when the shaman looked at him again.

"You talked with your mother about this?" Don Francisco asked.

"Yes, this morning."

"And your father knows about this?"

"He's gone to Paucartambo today."

"I see," Don Francisco grunted. He glanced at the door again. "What did your mother tell you?"

"She said that the black jaguar is here because of me," Juan said. The shaman raised his hand for him to wait. Perhaps his question had been too direct. The corners of Don Francisco's mouth twitched when he spoke toward the door.

"Come in," he said. "You can hear better from inside the house."

The heavy wooden door opened into the room. Rosa slipped through and pushed it shut behind her. She came over to her grandfather and kissed him on the cheek. The twinkle in the old man's eyes said that he was glad that she was there.

"Good morning, Abuelito," she said. Her casual tone contradicted the dark red that spread across her cheeks. She tucked her bangs behind her ears and greeted Juan politely without making eye contact. "I didn't know that you had company, Grandfather. I was on my way to see Alicia. I stopped by to see if you needed anything. With her baby so close to coming, Mother said that I could spend the day here instead of going to Paucartambo. I'm sure that..."

Her grandfather stopped her with a raised hand. "Rosita, pour yourself a cup of tea. I'm sure that Alicia can spare you for a few moments. Sit and visit with us."

He spoke with an odd formality, gesturing with an opened palm toward Juan. "It's agreeable with you that my granddaughter joins us?"

Juan nodded, acknowledging Rosa with a sideways glance. She held her cup in one hand, spread her skirt out with the other, and sat down next to him.

"So you are helping your friend Alicia today," her grandfather noted. "She is well, I trust."

"She is well, but the baby is large in her, and it's hard for her to take care of everything, with the house, the garden, and the cooking for her husband," Rosa said. "Her mother's helping out, but it's Alicia's first one. Doña Mariana already said that she wants me there when it's time to deliver the baby. She knows how high-strung Alicia is. I'll be able to soothe her better than anyone."

Her grandfather nodded. "Doña Mariana is a skilled medicine woman and a wise teacher. You can learn much from her. It's important for our people, for she's old and needs someone who can take over for her some day." He looked at Juan. "The birth of each child is important," he said, "and each one reminds us of that which we would like to forget, that new life comes forth to replace the old. The ancient ones called it the *pachacuti,* the never-ending spiral of time through which each generation travels."

"That's exactly what Doña Mariana said, Grandfather. She told me that each of us stands on the shoulders of those who have come before us," Rosa said.

"Just as we become the shoulders for those who follow us," Juan said. Rosa and her grandfather stared at him. His face suddenly felt warm. "My sister told me this when I was little," he mumbled. It felt like he was five years old again, except that Marta wasn't there.

The old man took pieces of a pipe from a cloth embroidered with a hummingbird in green and purple thread. The shaman wedged a long wooden stem into a bowl carved from dark green stone. He scraped it out with a jagged piece of bone. "It was your sister who gave me this pouch to hold my pipe," he said.

Juan looked down at the plump leaves that floated on the surface of his cup. He wasn't sure what to say. He had so many questions about Marta and about the jaguar. If only he could read the coca like the shaman. He glanced at Rosa, but her eyes were fixed on her grandfather. He looked at Don Francisco. The shaman's opaque eyes studied his face with eagle-like intensity. "What is it you want to know?" he said.

Juan sat his cup down and rubbed the scar in his hand. "My mother said you could tell me why the jaguar has come," he said.

The shaman nodded. "There is much to talk about. But I have a special tea that I make from the San Pedro cactus. It would be best to ask the plant's help in our discussions." He motioned to Rosa with his eyes, and she returned holding a sealed glass bottle and a small crystal glass. Don Francisco filled the glass to the brim with the light amber-colored liquid and prayed over it. "Ask the plant to cleanse you, to heal you, and to teach you," he said.

Juan took the glass from Rosa's hand and swallowed it in a single gulp. The bitter taste of the thick tea made him shiver. Don Francisco refilled the glass twice for Rosa and twice for himself. When he was finished, the shaman took a pinch of dry tobacco leaf and tamped it into the end of the pipe with a blackened thumb.

"Rosita, bring me some fire," he said. He lifted the pipe toward the corners of the room and chanted prayers to the four directions. Rosa grabbed a stick from the oven and held the red tip over the bowl. Her grandfather sucked until the tobacco crackled with flame.

Half-closed lids shrouded the shaman's eyes. He blew out a puff of smoke toward the ground. "The lower world is the *ukhupacha*, an inner world where those who seek to be medicine men and women must first travel," he said. "The serpent spirit Sachamama wraps her coils of light around them. Only when they face their own shadows can they serve those who come for help."

He blew another puff into the gray haze that hung in the room. "The middle world is the *kaypacha*, the world that we live in and the world in which we die," he said. Otorongo, the jaguar, teaches the shaman how to dance between life and death. It is the most rigorous of all teachers and must be treated with great respect. It suffers fools not at all."

He blew a puff of smoke toward the rafters. "The upper world is the *hanakpacha*, where the shaman travels to find wisdom that can be known but not told," he said. "Here is where Hatun Kuntur flies wingtip to wingtip with Spirit. Only with a strong heart does one see through the eyes of the condor and find his vision. It is a lonely and sometimes dangerous path to become a person of knowledge, and a medicine person learns to navigate the different worlds only by losing his way many times," Don Francisco said.

He laid the pipe across his lap. His lips moved with a wordless benediction, and he shifted his gaze between Juan and Rosa before he settled on his granddaughter. "Is it the path of the healer that you wish to travel?" he asked.

"I want this very much, Abuelito," she answered.

The shaman nodded toward Juan. "What about you? What are you looking for?"

Juan burped. The bitter taste of the San Pedro was strong in his mouth and made his saliva ropy. An uneasy feeling rumbled inside his stomach.

"Everything has happened so fast over the past few days," he said. "I don't know what to think anymore. When I asked my mother, she told me to talk to you."

"And?" Don Francisco said.

"It's about my sister," Juan blurted. "That black jaguar is a warning, isn't it?"

The shaman grabbed his staff and pulled himself up. Juan saw the hummingbird perched on top of the dark carved wood, its wingtips bridging the heads of the jaguar and the condor. A serpent, carved into the staff, hid its head underneath his hand. "Take off your hat and close your eyes," Don Francisco said.

Juan felt the tremble of the thin, bony hands against the sides of his head. The tips of jaguar claws dangled against the back of his neck. The shaman's whispered prayer was the wind at twilight after heavier gusts had died down. He felt the lips press against the top of his head. The warm breath blew with a loud whooshing sound, and the smell of tobacco smoke was strong. A hot, slender shaft of light pierced his crown. His eyes rolled back into his head.

64

Voices echoed inside a cave. A pounding drum pulled him deeper into the dark. A hummingbird sheathed in iridescent green feathers and with a mask of purple feathers guided him forward. Yellow coils writhed inside a steamy mist, and the jungle snake raised its triangular head. Shadowy beings with waist-length black hair circled around him, but their eyes were filled with too much light to see their faces. A jaguar's hoarse roar vibrated through him. He shivered in the icy waters of a mountain lagoon. A fish leaped out and turned into a skeleton. A man became a bird and soared over a stone hut nestled between snow-capped peaks.

Chapter Eleven

The shaman's medicine song asked the spirit of the San Pedro plant for healing and for cleansing. The rattle vibrated around Juan's head, and the words of the *icaro* came faster. He wiped the sweat from his face. The room was spinning. Nauseous waves of cramps twisted like a snake through his bowels. The sour taste of the plant rose from his stomach. "I'm going to be sick," he croaked.

Don Francisco handed him a clay pot. "Let it all come out. Not only the contents of your stomach, but empty out everything that troubles you," he said.

Juan grabbed onto the handles and purged until his stomach had nothing left. When he was finished, he sat back with his hands still wrapped around the pot. The shaman held a brown rattle in one hand and in the other a bottle of *agua de florida*. He took a sip and pursed his lips. Juan shut his eyes just before the spray hit his face with the pungent smell of flowers, herbs, and spices.

"Hear the voices of the ancient ones call your names," Don Francisco sang. "Feel their spirit singing in your bones. Listen to them call you to come and play. They say that it is the play that keeps you strong. It is the play that keeps you young. Hey, hey, come and play, little ones. Come and play, they say."

The shaman started around their shoulders and spun the gourd upward in a spiral, ending with a flourish of rattling above Juan and Rosa. "Open your hands," he said. Don Francisco poured the perfumed water into their hands. "Rub your hands, clap three times, and breathe it in deeply three times," he said. "Then sweep your hands down your body from head to foot to cleanse yourself."

Rosa's grandfather set the bottle down and picked up a condor feather with a silver tip. He flicked the long black wing feather with a series of sharp snaps, sweeping downward along their bodies with brisk strokes. When he was finished, he lowered himself back down onto his mat, nodding his head with satisfaction.

The vaporous alcohol and herb mixture of *agua de florida* burned inside Juan's nostrils. His stomach was still queasy, but it was his head that surprised him. He looked around the room with a strange, detached sort of clarity. The San Pedro cactus leaning against the wall and the plants stacked on the floor vibrated with a dim light. The colors of the tapestries on the wall were like bright pots of bubbling dye. A clear light hovered over Don Francisco's and Rosa's heads. He felt better than he had in days. There was nothing that he wanted to think about. It was enough just to sit there.

"Juanito, how are you?"

He trained his eyes on the shaman's face. "I'm better," he answered.

"Rosita?"

"I'm well, Abuelito," she said.

"Good. Bring me another stick from the fire," he said. He blew the smoke from the pipe underneath his hat and over himself. He handed the pipe to Rosa. "Smoke from it three times," he said. When she was done, the shaman nodded and pointed across the room. Her face beamed when she handed Juan the pipe.

The smoke tasted harsh and its smell was pungent. Juan swallowed hard to keep from coughing. It was *mapacho,* a strong tobacco from the jungle. The room wavered in a smoky haze. He handed the pipe back.

Don Francisco studied him for several moments before he shifted his attention to Rosa. "You are here together, but each of you has a different dream," he said. "And it is right that you choose your own path. But if your destinies are to be linked by a common thread, it will be found in what brings to you happiness. Only you know. Do you understand what I am saying?" he asked. He looked at each of them.

Rosa's eyes were bright with anticipation when she said yes. Juan wasn't sure where this was going, but he nodded. The shaman sorted through the bag of coca until he held three sets of three leaves in his hand. He handed a *k'intu* of coca leaves to Juan and another to Rosa.

"Three is the sacred number for the upper, the middle, and the lower worlds," the shaman said. He touched a finger to his forehead, to his chest, and to his belly. "These worlds correspond with three levels of perception: thinking, feeling, and being.

"Our belly is the *ukhupacha,* the place of emergence," he said. "It is our inner world, the world of being who we are. It is the place where earth and water first come together with the form and the formlessness of life energy.

"The world of the *kaypacha* is here," he said. He placed his hand over his solar plexus. "The middle world is the place of feeling who we are."

"Tell him about the heart, Abuelito," Rosa said.

The corners of her grandfather's eyes lifted and his face softened. "The heart is where the middle world meets the upper world," he said. "It is where the shaman finds his guidance. He listens for the voices of the ancestors. Q'inti, the hummingbird from the Sun, carries their words to those who are able to hear."

Juan wondered if this was what happened when someone's heart was broken. Maybe they couldn't hear this guidance so good. He asked his question before it was fully formed in his head. "How does one hear this bird?" he asked.

Rosa giggled before her grandfather stopped her with an unusual look of reproach. A warm feeling crept across Juan's cheeks. Don Francisco turned his attention back to him.

"It isn't about words or concepts but of instinct and intuition," he said. "It is a different kind of knowing. A shaman learns to perceive like the children and the beasts do but with awareness. Too soon, we are taught to bury our wisdom underneath words, worried about what others will say." The old man's eyes gentled with a look that Juan thought was reserved only for Rosa. "Do you understand?" he asked.

Yes, Juan said with his eyes. He understood what Don Francisco was saying. He felt that he was back in the pastures on the high plateau, listening to the shaman explain how all of nature worked together. He'd never thought about the stuff inside of him in this way.

"The *hanakpacha* is the upper world where the healer steps beyond personal power," Don Francisco said. He touched his crown. "That which blows from Spirit enters here," he said. "And it comes through our throat where we create our stories. This is why you must choose your words with great care. For the stories you tell are the ones that create your destiny."

He touched his brow with the tip of his index finger. "And this is the other eye through which the shaman learns to see."

Juan stared at Don Francisco. Maybe now the old man would explain how he had looked into the future and read the leaves at his baptism. "What do you mean by another eye and learning to see?" he asked.

The old man's bushy eyebrows knitted together. "When most people look, they see only the physical object and talk about its size, its shape, its color, and other details," he said. "A shaman looks into the space between things and searches for their relationship. This is how he dances with destiny outside of normal reality."

If he could have seen like this, he would have stayed home with Marta on his sixth birthday, and he would have left La Reina in the corral when he saw the jaguar that morning.

The corners of the shaman's mouth crinkled into a thin smile. "A healer uses his vision for more than just to keep himself safe. He uses it to create new possibilities for himself and for others. But the real question is how to create a future of your choosing," Don Francisco said. "Each healer must find their own way, one that works best for them. Destiny is not a destination. It is a journey that lasts a lifetime."

"But how can I see through a third eye to help other people?" Juan asked. He blinked several times, but the shaman's face remained fuzzy.

"You have to look at a person's body of light to see where help is needed," the shaman said.

"What does it look like?" he asked.

A harsh cough darkened Don Francisco's cheeks, deepening the lines in his face. He drained the last of his tea, picked up his pipe, and thumped the bowl. He scraped out the blackened residue of tobacco. "Rosita, set those candles in front of him, one beside the other," her grandfather said. He pointed to the shelf above Juan's head, where two candles sat burning. She jumped up and placed them on the floor. "Now, focus your eyes between the two flames until they become one," he said.

Juan sat and stared. Every time the light from the two candles began to merge, he would blink, and it would separate back into two flames again. "Soften your eyes more and look along the edges of the flames," Don Francisco said. "And try not to blink. Let me know when you are there."

His eyes began to water, but Juan didn't blink. Nothing happened at first. The flames jumped back and forth. He drew them closer together. He nodded.

He heard a high-pitched whistle. It was a *piruru*, a flute carved from the wing bone of a condor. Juan's forehead tingled, and the room shifted into wavy lines of dim light. He stared at where the shaman sat, but he saw only a smoky silhouette. The reddish-orange glow of his pipe slowly rose toward the rafters. Vertical lines of light vibrated in a transparent bubble around Don Francisco. He sat suspended in air. A thin, wispy funnel spun underneath him and others spun from his belly, his solar plexus, his chest, his throat, his brow, and the top of his head. Don Francisco was made of yellowish spinning wheels of light.

Even with his eyes closed, Juan could see it. Open or closed, it did not matter. After a few moments, the cloud disappeared, and the shaman was back on the floor. His eyes were rolled back into his head. Drooping lids shielded all but a small crescent of yellow sclera. He seemed to be looking directly into the *hanakpacha* itself.

A wisp of smoke curled upward from the pipe that rested between Don Francisco's hands. The movement of his chest was barely perceptible. Rosa stood with the flute in her hands. The worry in her face surprised Juan. He knew that what her grandfather had done was extraordinary. But it never occurred to him that it could be dangerous. The wind that whistled through the cracks of the house sounded mournful. A chill settled into the room.

The shaman's sudden jump startled Juan and Rosa. His eyelids fluttered open and he took a deep breath. His hands, covered with weathered, parchment-like skin, were tinged with blue when he lifted the pipe. Rosa took it away and helped him to his feet. She held the staff upright and told her grandfather to wrap his hands around it. With quick flicks of her wrist, she made the condor feather sound like a bird in flight when she circled around him, sweeping it down over his head, along his torso and legs, and down to his feet. Each pass ended with the silver tip tapping against the floor.

When she had finished with the feather, Rosa sipped from the bottle of *agua de florida* and misted the front of her grandfather three times from his feet to his head. She stepped behind him and misted him three times from his head to his feet. Then she took the staff and poured the flower-scented water into Don Francisco's hands. He cleansed himself and sat back down.

Juan stared at Rosa when she took her place next to him. It shouldn't have surprised him, but it did. Rosa was a shaman or at least a skilled apprentice. How much more did she know?

A loud sound shattered the silence. They both stared at Don Francisco, who looked equally surprised at his prodigious belch. Juan's eyes widened and he looked at Rosa. She stared back at him, her eyebrows arched. A wicked gleam danced in her eyes. She stuck out her tongue, stretched out the corners of her mouth with her fingers, and crossed her eyes.

Juan never had a chance. Tears welled up, and green coca tea spewed from his nose. He could hardly breathe. Rosa clapped her hands and giggled. She shrieked when he fell over on her and dug his fingers into her side. One would barely stop laughing before the other started it up again. Don Francisco sat his cup down and wiped his face. Tears streamed down his cheeks. He was laughing too.

Chapter Twelve

Everything looked and felt different when he and Rosa walked between the river and the rolling hills that bordered the village. Even button-sized yellow flowers that grew flush with the ground vibrated with tiny swirls of light. His finger tingled when he touched the petals. A dry wind swirled around them when they stopped on a hillside that overlooked the village, reddening their cheeks and coating them with a layer of dust. Juan marveled how the sky could be dark blue and filled with the blinding radiance of a white sun at the same time. The peaks of Ausangate sparkled with crystalline light. Thin clouds raced across a vibrating horizon. Wind blew through a grove of eucalyptus trees and waxy green leaves shimmered with light.

Rosa shouted and pointed to the sky. Two Andean eagles circled above, rising on the afternoon thermals. White highlighted the underside of long, honey-brown wings and short tail feathers. Only the tips of the wings, buffeted by the wind, moved. A hazy blue-gray circle of light radiated around each bird. One eagle folded its wings and dove toward them. Just before it reached the ground, its feathers flared out, and it climbed back up.

Rosa clapped her hands. "We are eagles and we fly wingtip to wingtip. We'll soar across the *altiplano* to the highest of the mountains, Apu Ausangate," she shouted. Caught in a funnel of wind, she threw her head back and spun with her arms outstretched, her black braid whipping against the burgundy sweater. Juan grabbed her wrist with his hand, leaned away from her, and they spun around in a circle. It was like when he was a boy, playing with Rosa and his sister. He was happy in a way that he hadn't thought was possible again.

When they could spin no more, they hung onto each other, laughing and gasping for air. Her arms reached up around his neck. Her breath smelled of *muña*, and the smell of *agua de florida* scented her hair. He felt the beat of her heart against his chest. A yearning flooded into him that he had never felt before. He jumped when he heard the girls giggle behind him. His two sisters swung a basket of plants and herbs between them. Their eyes widened when they saw the look on his face.

When he stepped toward them, they shrieked and ran back toward the village. Short black braids that stuck out from behind bounced with each step. They flew down the hill, plants spilling from their basket. Several women looked up to see what all the fuss was about. Juan watched his sisters disappear into the dusty streets below. Rosa laughed so hard that she fell onto the ground.

"It's not funny," he said.

"Come and sit down," she said.

He slumped down beside her. "You don't understand. My mother worries me to death with all her questions," he said. "Just this morning, she asked me about the dance. The whole village could hear her. She doesn't know how loud she talks sometimes."

Rosa lifted a suspicious eyebrow. "And?" she said.

"She embarrasses me," Juan said. He folded his arms across his chest and looked down at the village. When he glanced over at Rosa, he saw the frown on her face. "I'm not that good of a dancer, and I've forgotten most of the steps," he said.

She smiled and ran her hand through his bangs. "After we shear off some of this, I'll show you the steps," she said. "I've got a feeling that your feet will move just fine to the music. But we'll have to see if they can move fast enough to keep up with mine."

Rosa jumped up and ran toward the village. She was bent over laughing when Juan caught up with her. He grabbed her underneath the arms and spun her around.

"We'll see about who can keep up," he said. "But for now, I'll walk you to Alicia's. She's expecting you."

Rosa's eyes widened with mock surprise. "Are you sure we should be seen walking together?" she asked.

Juan grabbed her arm. "Come on, I've got to get back home," he said. "My mother will have already heard the news from my sisters. It will be harder than ever to keep her nose out of my business now."

He wanted to talk to Rosa about her grandfather. When he had tried to talk to him after the ceremony, the shaman had sidestepped his questions. He told him that all would be revealed at the right time. There was more that Juan needed to know first, Don Francisco had said. Much more.

"Your grandfather told me to pay attention to the everyday things," Juan said. "He spoke about other fields that had to be harvested first before he could teach me anything more. What do you think he meant?"

"Ever since I was a little girl, he's taught me to see that the world is made of light," Rosa said. "He says that light is the life force of creation. It's in everything. But you need to see and feel it before he can teach you to work with it."

Juan felt his hands tingle. His mother had taught him how to lay his hands on animals to help them. He wondered if this is what Rosa meant.

"There is much to learn, and I'm glad that you want to understand these things," she said. "It's important that his knowledge isn't lost when he crosses over. I know that this weighs heavy on him. He worries whether there will be enough of us to pass on the wisdom of the ancient ones to the children. And I worry about him. He puts on a brave front, but his health hasn't been the best over the past few years. Both he and Doña Mariana need to slow down."

"But there are other shamans in the communities around Paucartambo," Juan said.

"My grandfather said that many have passed on and that there are only a few like him around anymore. It takes years of study to learn how to work with the light."

"You must have learned a lot from him," Juan said. It was obvious from the ceremony that she knew a lot more than she let on. She even spoke like her grandfather when he tried to get a direct answer.

"He and Doña Mariana have taught me much, and he has it in his heart for you and me to take their places when they cross over," Rosa said. "That ceremony was a very special thing he did for us."

Her words excited and scared Juan at the same time. He
thought that dream had died with Marta. But what had
happened inside Rosa's grandfather's house was pure magic.
It was a glimpse into another world, a place where ordinary rules
did not apply. His eyes had been opened to see in a new way.
Never had he felt more alive. But what would he have to do to
follow the shaman's path? He'd already learned a lot about the
plants and healing from his mother. How long would it take
before he could do what Don Francisco did?

"Don't worry," Rosa said. "You'll see. My grandfather says
that with Spirit all things are possible." She laughed at the
puzzled look on his face. Just like his mother, Rosa answered
his questions before he asked them. When they walked back
through the village, he felt the eyes of the people on them. The
same mother stood in the open doorway of her home, nursing
the baby in her arms. The toddler pulled at her skirts. He
smiled at her, and she smiled back.

Rosa squeezed his hand. "That's the baby who is being
baptized tomorrow at the festival," she said. "My grandfather
wants us to help with the ceremony."

"I don't know about that" he said.

"You don't want to?" she said.

"It would make my mother happy, but it's my father I'm
worried about. He's not going to like it one bit when he hears
that I talked to your grandfather today. He'd be furious if I were
to help Don Francisco, even with a baptism."

"I'll talk to your mother," Rosa said. "She'll convince him.
Everyone will be there, all dressed up. The baptism is after the
ceremony for the land. There's all the food and drink and,
of course, there will be music and the dance afterward. It will
be so much fun," she said. She stood in a dancing pose and
extended her hands. "My grandfather says that if we are to be
medicine people, it's important for the village to see us help at
the baptism. It's the community that will decide if we are to be
healers." Juan tried to speak, but Rosa kept talking. "I'll help
you with the dance steps after I see Alicia. I'll come get you when
I'm done."

She put her hand on his arm, and they stopped in front of the same women that he'd seen weaving earlier. An old woman washed the alpaca wool with the root *saqtana*. The little girls that stirred the open pots of dye smiled shyly. He remembered when they used to go with Marta to gather the ingredients for the different colors. His sister had taught them how to pick the tiny bugs called *cochunillas* from cactus without getting pricked. They would grind them into a dark vermillion powder to make the red dye. Their mother had to ferment the *cochonilla* and *motemote* plants together for a month to make the light blue dye. The brown colors came from a moss called *kcaka sunca* that grew in the rocks. They picked the leaves from an herb called *colpa* to make green.

It took their father several days of hiking in the mountains to find a root called *cheqche* to make the yellow dye. He would also bring back *sal,* a salt that he found in volcanic dirt. It was to fix the colors and to create different shades. The orange came from berries that he picked when the men harvested the coca leaf in the jungle. Marta used to paint their faces with them, and they would run around and scream that they had stared at the sun for too long.

Rosa joked with the little girls about who was the best weaver. Each insisted that she made the best hat bands and belts. They said that when they turned fifteen, their mothers would teach them patterns handed down from their grandmothers to weave blankets, tapestries, and clothes. When she asked them which colors they liked best, the girls laughed and said that they liked reds and yellows best because they were happy colors. Their mothers used black and blue when they felt sad, they said.

The women wore broad smiles when Rosa and Juan walked past, but they kept their hands busy moving the shuttles back and forth. Their eyes crinkled, and they winked at each other. "How wonderful young love is," Juan overheard one of the older women say.

"But it only happens to the young," her friend laughed back. The older girls, spinning dyed strands of yarn around their spindles, whispered to one another and pointed toward Juan and Rosa. The little girls giggled and pointed at their big sisters.

Chapter Thirteen

It was too early for the cracking of branches and the smell of burning eucalyptus, Juan thought. His father must have had a rough night. Whenever he couldn't sleep, he'd be up earlier than usual. He stayed beneath the blankets and watched Humberto stoke the oven fire. Light flickered across his father's face, and his shadow wandered across the stone wall. A thin column of steam hissed from the spout of the blackened kettle, but he seemed unaware of it. When he had returned from Paucartambo last night, Wilhelmita had told him about Juan's visit with Don Francisco and the baptism. There was a big argument, and his father had nothing to say to him after that.

When the water came to a rolling boil, Juan slipped out from between the covers and got dressed. The tight weave of the natural gray fibers of baby alpaca wool was stiff across his shoulders. His mother had put in the final stitches in the black trim last night. Rosa's haircut made the matching peaked hat feel too loose on his head, but he decided that it would look better to let the cords hang along the sides of his face. He walked over to the oven and set the kettle off to the side.

His father rubbed something between his fingers, but Juan couldn't see what it was. He thought about how big his hands had seemed when he was little. They'd been roughened from years of exposure to dry cold and the intense sunlight of the *altiplano*. The cracks, crevices, and calluses had come from a lifetime of tilling, planting, and harvesting. But he knew that the misshapen fingertips hadn't come from farming. It was from frostbite, but his father never talked much about how that happened. He had gotten lost in the mountains once was all he would say.

Humberto stared into the fire with not even a glance his way. He looked surprised when Juan set a cup of tea beside him. He tucked his hands underneath his arms and stared back into the reddish-orange embers, his dark eyes lost in thought. Juan remembered how Marta and he would wake up early and stand next to him by the fire. His father could make tiny animals carved of stone disappear and then pull them out from their ears. When the grounds were covered with snow, he told them stories about his adventures in the Cordillera Vilcanota. He had traveled through the mountain range often when he was a young man, working with an uncle who was a trader. But the one mountain that Humberto never talked about was Ausangate.

Juan pulled on the cords from his hat, wishing that his father would say something. He was eighteen. Today Juan Eduardo Del Gato would stand before the community of San Mateo and receive his own land. It was what he and his father had been working toward these past five years. It was one of the few times when everyone in the village put aside their work and celebrated. The traders would set up their booths. There'd be all sorts of food, especially *cuye*. The head from the roasted guinea pig was his father's favorite part. And, of course, there would be plenty of *chicha* to drink.

Unspoken feelings hung like smoke in the room, and there would never be a better time for them to talk. He needed to explain about his visit with Don Francisco. The baptism was for Rosa's sake, he wanted to tell him. Farming had made a good life for their family, and it would make a good one for him too. His father needed to understand that. His words faded on his lips when he saw the furrow deep between Humberto's thick eyebrows. His father's weathered face, red from the fire, looked worn and tired. But he had to talk with him, one man to another. And it was best to do it before the rest of the family got up. Juan cleared his throat. "I went to see Don Francisco because…"

"Because why?" Humberto said. His eyes reflected the firelight. "What did that old man tell you? Are you to be the next shaman for our people? Is it your destiny to find the Snow Star? Of course, he told you about your *hatun karpay*, your journey of initiation to Ausangate. What other tales has Don Francisco ladled into your head, boy? Tell me. I want to know."

He stared at his father's toes, also misshapen from frostbite. He'd never seen him this angry before. Humberto shoved his fingers in front of his face. "Take a good look at my hands also," he insisted. "Not a day goes by that I don't wake up and feel the pain until I fall asleep at night. Even then, the throbbing wakes me up. And you know what? I count myself lucky to be alive, no thanks to Don Francisco. When I came down off of that mountain, I was crawling. Do you hear me, boy? Crawling like an animal on my hands and knees. I would have died if your mother hadn't found me on the trail when she did."

"But Papá," he said.

Humberto dropped his voice to a hiss when the children began to stir under the covers. "And for what?" he said. "I was young like you and I, too, believed in the old man's foolish stories. He told me that the greatness of those who would be healers was measured by how they faced challenges on their journey of initiation. In order to be a truly worthy medicine man, I had to travel to Apu Ausangate, the most powerful of mountains in the Cordillera Vilcanota. We'd hold a ceremony for Spirit to be with me, to guide my journey, and to keep me safe from harm, he said."

Juan buried his hands under his poncho. He understood why his mother didn't want to tell him about his father and Don Francisco before. When he looked up, he saw the pain welling in his father's eyes. His fist opened around a delicately shaped condor, carved from black onyx. "Other than my hands and feet, this is all I have left to show," he said. "I had it gripped so tight that your mother couldn't pry it out of my hand when she found me. It was to guide me to the Snow Star." His father picked up a stick and tried to shove several pieces of crumbling embers together. Snaps and pops punctuated the silence.

"What happened?" Juan finally said. "I know how much you traveled with your uncle through the mountains when you were a young man. You can still trek faster and longer than anyone else in the village."

Humberto's voice lowered. "Being strong and fast is not nearly enough for Ausangate. It is a different kind of mountain. This *apu* has a spirit that wants all of you, heart and soul. You cannot imagine." He picked up his cup and sipped the coca tea.

"I wanted so much to reach the Snow Star," he said. "I knew that it would be dangerous. But I was young and, like you said, I was strong in the mountains. The old man had told me that Ausangate's summit was a gateway to the *hanakpacha*. There was where I would find Hatun Kuntur, he said. It was the condor who carried the shaman into the upper world. Riding on its back, I would soar wingtip to wingtip with Spirit and receive my vision."

"What happened?" Juan asked.

His father sat the cup down and rubbed his hands over the fire. "When I reached the summit, there was no Snow Star. I was lucky that your mother found me when she did. I was in pretty rough shape for the first few weeks. Wilhelmita took me into her and her mother's home and tended to me day and night. I had nowhere else to go. My parents had died when I was young, and the uncle who raised me had crossed over the previous winter."

"Didn't Don Francisco offer to help?"

Humberto shrugged his shoulders and picked his tea back up. "After my return to the village, he tried to talk with me. I blamed him for my failure. It was a fool's errand, I told him. I stayed with Wilhelmita and her mother until we got married and built our own home," he said. "I put the past behind me, and your mother and I worked hard to make a good life together. When you were born, we were the family that I had hoped for. I had a son who would work alongside of me in the fields and help provide for our family and then someday for one of his own."

"But not everything worked out the way you planned, did it?" Juan said.

Humberto acted surprised by the question. He tilted his head to one side, as though he was seeing Juan for the first time. "Go ahead," he said. "What do you want to say?"

"When I was little, you'd sit me and Marta on your knees, and you'd tell us stories about Pachamama and Inti Taita," he said. "You said that Mother Earth and Father Sun were in love, just like you and Mamá. It was love that held everything together, you said. But things went wrong when Marta died. After she was gone, you hardly spoke to me. I understand why you would blame me for her death. But I thought that I could make it up to you someday. Maybe if I was a good farmer like you, then you'd be proud of me. I never meant to go behind your back to talk to Don Francisco. It's just that I didn't know what to think anymore, and I knew that you didn't want to talk about that jaguar."

His father opened his mouth, but Juan stopped him. "For the first time since Marta's death, my life might mean something more than trying to forget the past," he said. "But I have to find my own way with it. Why can't you see that? Is it such a bad thing to want to follow my own dream? I'm sorry that you're angry with me, and I'm sorry that I'm not what you wanted for a son. But it was me who went to talk to Don Francisco. He didn't come to me. He didn't know that…"

His father stopped him. "Maybe it shouldn't matter what happened between me and the old man," he said. "But I don't want you to make the mistakes that I did." He rubbed his face as though it could take away the painful memories. Juan saw a grief etched in the deep lines of his father's face that he had not noticed before. The anguish in his eyes scared him more than the anger. Maybe he'd opened a door that should have stayed shut.

"And I'm sorry for the hurt that you've carried about your sister," Humberto said. "I blame myself for what happened. I should have known better than to let her take the herd out that day. But that storm came faster than I could've imagined. When I heard the rumble of thunder, I was sure that your sister would be back soon. I thought you were playing with Rosa. But her father said that he had seen you with your sister, and the two of you were driving the herd up to the high pastures. He thought it strange, but he figured that I told you it was okay."

Juan squirmed. He had lied to his father.

"When you and Marta didn't come home that afternoon," his father said, "I went up with a couple of men from the village. We saw the herd scattered across the pasture, heading toward home. It took us a while to find you. I shouted your names and kept calling you. I finally found you huddled between several boulders. Your face was scratched and dirty, and your clothes and your hair were singed from lightning. You were shaking when I picked you up. You must have still been in shock. I told you that I had come to take you home." His father stared at his hands. "You hid your face," he said.

"The look on your mother's face when she saw Marta's body..." His father shuddered. "She struggled for months afterward. It was all I could do just to get her out of bed some days. For the longest time, you would barely talk to me. I tried to keep things going and did what I could, hoping that things would smooth out between us. The last few years, I thought that you had found some peace working in the fields with me." Humberto's voice faltered and then stopped.

Juan stared at the leaves in the bottom of his cup. It was the first time they had spoken about Marta's death. He had wanted to talk, but he never imagined it would be about the day of the storm.

"I've never wanted you to follow the path of the shaman, much less be an apprentice to Don Francisco," Humberto said. "I didn't trust him, and I have been afraid of what might happen," his father said. Hissing steam rose from the coals when he tossed the last of his tea into the fire.

"But why would you be afraid?" asked Juan.

His father rubbed the condor between his hands. "I'd be afraid that I would find your body lying on that mountain someday. I would rather die than lose another child, especially you," he said.

Chapter Fourteen

Dressed in a poncho of deep vermillion and wearing a beaded cap crowned with scarlet macaw feathers from the jungle, Don Francisco reminded Juan of a picture of an Inca priest that he had once seen in a schoolmaster's history book of Peru. Doña Mariana, wearing a new short-brimmed white hat and a red poncho decorated with the Southern Cross, stood next to the shaman. The council of village elders formed a half-circle next to them. The young men and women stood next to their parents in front. Juan gave his mother a sideways glance when she squeezed his arm, and he stopped playing with the cords that hung down from his hat. He had been telling her what each elder said. His lips moved slowly to make sure she understood. The last elder reminisced about when she had received her own land and what it had meant to her. The woman reminded the new land owners that it would take a husband's and wife's share to support a family. He cut his eyes over at Rosa, and she smiled back. His face flushed when his mother patted his back.

When Juan was called to receive his land, his mother and his father stepped forward with him. His property would be two new fields near the top of Inkawari Mountain. The climb would be good for such a strong young man he was told. The crowd laughed. Each member of the village council shook his hand and embraced him with a formal hug. Humberto handed him the new hoe and scythe that he had bought in Paucartambo. José and his sisters gathered around him afterwards. His brother offered to hold his new tools for him during the baptism.

After a short break, the family came forward with their baby for the baptism. Don Francisco nodded at Juan and Rosa to come up. He had Juan stand by his side. Rosa stood next to Doña Mariana. The family stood in front. The mother folded back the corner of the alpaca blanket from the baby's face. The heat was already strong in the cloudless day. The father held a squirming toddler on his hip.

"In the harshness of the highlands, too many times we grieve the loss of a newborn," Don Francisco said. "But today we celebrate a baby girl, a gift to the parents and to our village. As the wind from Apu Ausangate blows through San Mateo, so does the breath of Spirit pass through this little one." He chanted and shook his rattle over the girl. Juan's lips moved with the shaman's when he called to Apus Inkawari, Ausangate, Ocongate, Machu Picchu, Huayna Picchu, Salcantay, and the other guardian mountains. He whispered the names of the serpent, the jaguar, the condor, and the hummingbird.

Rosa helped Doña Mariana down so she could rest her hand on the earth. With a lump of coca leaves tucked inside her cheek, the old woman warbled when she spoke. "Pachamama," she said, "you are the blood of our blood, the bone of our bone, and the Spirit of our Spirit. May this child walk in harmony with the plants, the stones, the two-legged, the four-legged, and all sentient beings. May she walk in beauty on your belly."

She pushed herself up and raised her hand toward the sun. "Inti Taita you bring the light that gives life to the earth and to all beings," she said. "Mamaquilla, Grandmother Moon, you guide the seasons of growth. Star Brothers and Star Sisters, you lead us through the *pachacuti,* the spiral of endless time. Illa Tici Viracocha, Great Spirit, you have a thousand names and yet you are nameless. May you flow through this child like water flows from Ausangate."

She handed Rosa a knife carved of black obsidian. The villagers circled around and watched her cut a locket of hair from the baby's head and lay it on a white blanket. Everyone clapped and crowded around the parents to visit. The people dropped coins on the blanket for the baby.

Buckets of *chicha* were brought out to begin the celebration. Men who had set aside their hoes for the day readied their instruments. Hand-held *tinya* drums and dried llama hooves strung together on leather cords rattled with a shrill, clacking sound. Large hide-covered *wankaras* pounded with a deep, staccato rhythm. Ancient wind instruments, *antaras, sikus,* and *zamponas,* carried the different sounds of the wind that gusted through the mountain highlands.

Tapping his toe to the music, Juan finished his *chicha* and got back in line for more. He wouldn't get to see Rosa again until the dancing started. A friend of his mother shook her finger at him, but she laughed and filled his cup from a bucket of the sour corn beer. His friend Pepe challenged him to see who could empty theirs first. The other young men cheered when they finished in a tie. They refilled their cups and sang mournful ballads about failed crops and lost love to the haunting deep notes of the wooden flutes and panpipes. They followed the playful, high-pitched notes with songs about young love and abundant harvests. When Juan heard the high-pitched whistle of the *piruru,* the flute carved from the wing bone of an Andean condor, he drained his cup. It was time for the dance.

Voices called out to each other over the music. Boys grabbed the hands of girls dressed in colorful skirts and sweaters. Villagers gathered around the dancers. They laughed and shouted out encouragement. Juan spotted Rosa and stood next to her with the other couples inside the dance circle marked by white stones. Decked in a bright red skirt and jacket, she wore a padded black hat with white fringe along the border. In the custom of single women, she had her hat tilted to the side. She tossed her braid, plaited with crimson yarn, over her shoulder and held out her hand. With coppery cheeks tinged with red and lips that glistened in the morning light, Rosa Maria had to be the most beautiful girl in San Mateo. She locked her eyes onto his. He took her hand and slid his arm around her waist.

Their feet moved in unison to the beat of the drums. Easy on her feet, she glided under his outstretched hand and then back again to his side. He danced the steps that they had practiced yesterday after her visit with her friend Alicia, gaining confidence with each song. The crowd and the musicians spurred the couples on. He promenaded Rosa inside the circle of stones. His mother beamed at him and waved. She made sure that

Humberto did too. Faster and faster the drummers pounded the *wankaras* and the musicians blew their wooden panpipes. Villagers stood outside the ring, handing cups of *chicha* to the dancers when they passed by. Applause and shouts rang out when one couple and then another stumbled outside the white rocks, laughing and out of breath. Juan's new poncho was wet with perspiration when he and Rosa were left inside the circle, standing next to Pepe and his dance partner.

The villagers whistled and clapped. Juan wiped the sweat from his eyes and grabbed Rosa's hand. She whispered into his ear. "We are eagles," she said. They leaned out from each other, spinning in a tight circle with their other hand stretched toward the cheering crowd. They were soaring across the highlands. The faster the music played, the faster they spun. Rosa glistened in the afternoon sun. He saw the passion in her eyes. They were eagles and they would always fly together.

She shouted for him to slow down, but it was too late. His fingers slipped from her wrist, and he fell into the arms of the crowd. Rosa stumbled forward, landing on the ground. She lay on her side, her red skirt bunched up around her knees. The musicians stopped playing with a confusion of whistles, squeaks, and uneven beats. Juan shook her shoulder. "Rosa, are you okay?" he said. Her breathing was shallow. He rolled her onto her back. A red gash opened up her forehead, and a thin trickle of blood ran from the corner of her mouth. The white stone next to her head was smeared with crimson.

Juan picked her up and searched for her grandfather. But he was nowhere to be seen. Both sets of parents pushed their way through the crowd to reach him. Rosa's mother probed her neck for a pulse and put a hand on her chest. "Hush up," she told her husband. "He is being careful."

With her parents beside him, Juan carried Rosa inside their home and laid her on a straw mat. Her father propped her up on pillows and covered her with a blanket. Her mother cleaned the edges of the ragged cut with a damp cloth and wiped the dirt from her face. She tied a strip of muslin around Rosa's forehead. Fresh bleeding seeped into the makeshift bandage. Rosa's father looked at Juan. Juan dropped his eyes. His new poncho, stained with blood, looked dirty and worn. Her mother grabbed his arms. "Go find her grandfather," she said.

Wilhelmita's eyes were fixed on his lips when Juan stepped outside. "It's my fault," he said. "I shouldn't have swung her so hard."

His mother wiped his face with her handkerchief. "Stop it," she said. "It was an accident. Now go find Francisco José," she said.

"We'll wait for you at home," said Humberto.

Juan ran through the streets of San Mateo. He would tell Don Francisco what happened. The shaman would know what to do. He would make sure that Rosa would be okay. He had to.

Chapter Fifteen

The shadows of the dwindling day covered the front of Rosa's house when Juan returned. The wind, gusting through the streets, darkened his poncho with another layer of dirt. The clouds around Ausangate's peak were stained red. Otorongo, the jaguar that ate the light of the dying sun, was feeding now. Juan tried to push the bad thoughts out of his head. He had found Don Francisco at the family's home whose child was baptized today. The shaman had to stop at his house, but he said that he would be here soon.

Voices rose from inside the house. Juan leaned his ear against the door. Rosa's mother was shouting. Her husband tried to reason with her, but the tone of her voice left no room for misunderstanding. "We are not taking Rosa to Paucartambo," she said. "Not until my father has a chance to look at her."

"But there is a doctor there," Rosa's father said.

"I don't care if Paucartambo has a hundred doctors. It's too far," she said.

"I heard that this doctor came from a school in Cusco," he said. "He will know about modern medicines."

"For all that's sacred, I'd think that you would realize how important her grandfather is to Rosa," answered her mother. "He'll be here any moment. And he's been healing people in this village before you and I were born."

Startled by the hand on his shoulder, Juan jumped. Don Francisco's opaque eyes flashed a look of impatience. "If we don't get in there, we might lose our patient to a doctor in Paucartambo," he said. The shaman tapped on the door with his staff and pushed it open. He knelt by his granddaughter's side. Her mother looked up and motioned to Juan.

"Come in," she said. Rosa's father opened his mouth, but her mother grabbed his arm before he could say anything. "We need to go tell Doña Mariana," she told her husband. "My father will want her to fix a poultice. I heard that Alicia has gone into labor. She's probably there." When her husband started to protest, she pushed him toward the door. "He doesn't want you watching over his shoulder," she said. Juan glanced back. Rosa's mother stood in the doorway with her hand over her mouth before she stepped outside and pulled the door shut behind her.

Rosa's face was pale, and a bluish tinge colored her lips. Her grandfather nestled his fingers into the side of her neck. When he took the strip of cloth off of her forehead, it was mostly clotted blood between the swollen edges of the jagged wound. That there was no fresh bleeding didn't bode well, Juan thought. The sour taste of *chicha* crawled up into his mouth. "Is she going to be okay?" he asked. Don Francisco shot him a grim look and opened the top of his shoulder bag.

The shaman pulled out his rattle, a bottle of flower water, the condor feather, the pouch with his pipe, and a neatly wrapped bundle. Juan recognized the red alpaca cloth with black lightning bolts. Don Francisco had it with him at the baptism ceremony. It was his *mesa*. Inside were *q'uyas* that he used for healing, but Juan had never seen the special stones and crystals before. Rosa's grandfather unfolded the bundle and spread the cloth in front of him, smoothing out the wrinkles. He worked with a fluid, rapid movement. He picked up each *q'uya* and whispered words that were too faint to hear. He placed four shells around the corners, each carved with the fierce face of a warrior.

When he was finished, a transparent quartz crystal shaped into a condor sat at the top of his *mesa*. A half-polished and half-rough jaguar's head carved from black volcanic rock was in the middle. A heart-shaped crystal sat next to the jaguar. A coiled serpent of dark green stone lay at the bottom. A thin white flute sat on the left side of the medicine cloth, and a black obsidian knife lay on the right. A short staff with the figure of a jungle shaman carved into the top of the dark wood rested against the top of the red cloth.

Don Francisco took a sip from the bottle of *agua de florida* and misted the flower essence over the *q'uyas*. Sagging lids hid his eyes, and his lips moved silently. He picked up the pink heart crystal, pressed it against his mouth, and laid it on Rosa's chest. He shook the rattle and sang an *icaro*. He sang to the serpent, the jaguar, the hummingbird, and the condor. He sang to the mountains, the rivers, the earth, the sun, the moon and the stars, and to All That Is. The rattle's sound filled the room until even the stone walls seemed to vibrate. But Rosa's chest was still, and her lips were still tinged with blue. Juan looked at the shaman, but his eyes were closed.

She was dead.

His hand trembled when he touched Rosa. The cold, sick feeling twisted inside his stomach. He had done this, and he wasn't six years old anymore. That he was sorry wouldn't bring her back. He wanted to scream. How could something so perfect have gone so wrong? It was him, of course. It had to be him. It had been the same with Marta. He was cursed. Death came to those he loved, and it would always be his fault. He would go to Paucartambo, maybe even Cusco. No one there would know who he was or what he had done. He looked at the door.

Without opening his eyes, Don Francisco rested his hand on Juan's leg. The thin, bony fingers squeezed his knee. "Pray," he said.

The evening breeze blew between the cracks of the house. Juan took a deep breath and closed his eyes. Jumbled images of the jaguar's yellow eyes, copper-red faces framed with long black hair, and Rosa's pale skin and blue lips cascaded through his head. *Please come back,* he prayed. When he heard the eerie sound, he thought that it was the wind or one of the musicians from the dance. The clear notes brought him back to the room. It was the shaman who played the flute carved from a condor bone. His melody was inviting and then it was compelling. Juan saw light from the heart-shaped crystal shimmer over Rosa's chest. The light pulsed to the notes of the flute until it ran the length of her body. When the music ended, the shaman picked up the dark wooden staff, cleansed it with *agua de florida*, and handed it to him.

"This is a *chunta*," he said. "Our ancestors used it in healing ceremonies to break up the heavy energy around a person. Hit the floor around Rosa with the end. Go three times to the left and three times to the right. Make the earth shake." Juan held the staff with both hands and raised it up. The *chunta* was heavier than he thought it would be.

"Wait until I tell you to start," Don Francisco said and picked up his rattle. He sang an *icaro* to the ancient ones from Ausangate, asking them to work through Juan's hands. The *chunta* grew warm and Juan's hands tingled. "Now," Don Francisco said. Each time Juan struck the floor, the shaman sang louder. Juan's hands and his feet vibrated. They still tingled even when he was finished and the rattle and the singing had stopped. The space around Rosa was clearer, but her chest remained still. He laid the *chunta* back across the top of the red cloth.

Don Francisco held a stick from the fire over the green bowl of his pipe. "Blow the smoke from her feet to her head three times," he said. Juan blew until the yellow light around Rosa touched the walls. His sister had told stories about the gilt-lined Inca temples that reflected the light of a candle a thousand times. Rosa's house had become such a place. When he looked back at her, he saw a shadow over her forehead, a dark slit in an otherwise luminous shroud.

Her grandfather placed his hands on each side of her face, and he pressed his mouth against her forehead. The animal-like noise made Juan queasy. It sounded like a dog gulping down the afterbirth from a new-born alpaca. When he saw the shaman's barrel-shaped chest heave, he grabbed a pot from the side of the oven and held it to his face. After he had finished purging, Don Francisco pushed it away. Juan almost dropped the clay pot. The gaping wound on Rosa's forehead had turned into a thin red line. What kind of power could do such a thing?

"Take the bottle of *agua de florida* and spray a mist over her," the shaman rasped. "Start at her head and go down to her feet. Do it three times, and then go from her feet to her head three times." The strong herbal and alcohol essence burned Juan's mouth, and he spit it out. "I said a mist, not a bath. Take a smaller sip. Keep it between your teeth and lips and then blow," Don Francisco said. Juan misted it over Rosa twice more. "Good," said her grandfather, "and now that you have grounded her, lift her up three times." When Juan finished, he saw dark squiggly lines that drifted through the light over Rosa. It was an outline of her body, and it floated above her. The shaman took the bottle from his hand and handed him the condor feather.

"Sweep from her head to her feet three times," he said. "Then three times from her feet to her head. Do it now." Juan swept the black wing feather over her with a flick of his wrist like he had seen Rosa do for her grandfather, making a sound like the flapping of a condor's wings. When he had finished, the light was clear and ran in waves over her. He laid the feather back on the shaman's *mesa*.

All of Don Francisco's attention was focused on his granddaughter. The shaman tapped his finger on the heart-shaped crystal that rested on her chest. His lips moved with silent supplications. Only the wind that whistled past the stone house and the burning eucalyptus made any noise in the house. Once more he tapped the crystal.

Juan tried to imagine that Rosa's lips were somehow less blue, but her hand was cold when he touched it. When her grandfather took her hands, his eyes were moist. His voice was no longer guttural but child-like and soft. He sang a lullaby that Juan's mother sang to his little sisters when she tucked them in at night. "The ancestors watch over their children. They bring them home when they are lost," he sang. "See the ancient ones dancing in the wind, dancing in the wind. They come from the sacred mountain, dancing in the wind." He tapped the pink crystal a third time and it trembled. Juan was sure of it. He touched it with his finger. Tiny swells moved it up and down.

"Don Francisco," he said. "Look." The crystal rose higher with each breath that Rosa took. Her lips gained a touch of color and her cheeks pinked up. She took several deep breaths before her eyelids fluttered open. She gave her grandfather a sleepy smile.

"Are you okay, Abuelito?" she said.

Don Francisco wiped his eyes with the back of his hand and nodded. He took the crystal from her chest and tucked the edges of the blanket around her. He touched his lips to his granddaughter's forehead. Her eyes were clear and innocent, like a newborn's opened for the first time.

Rosa touched her forehead. "I remember now," she said. "It was the dance. I fell, didn't I?"

Juan held her hand to his chest. "You're okay," he said.

Rosa smiled. "I dreamed that I was flying," she said. "There were these people. Their faces were filled with light, but..."

Her grandfather touched his finger to her lips. "You can tell us later," he said. "It's important that you rest for now. Doña Mariana will be here soon with a poultice for your head. It will keep the swelling down. I don't want you to do anything for the next three days. You have to rest. And no more dancing for a while," he said. Rosa smiled and nodded.

Cool air rushed into the room. Rosa's parents stepped through the doorway with Doña Mariana behind them. Don Francisco's bushy eyebrows lifted when he looked at Juan. His eyes crinkled upwards, and his lips spread into a boyish grin. The shaman squeezed his shoulder. Juan wanted to thank him a thousand times over and tried to say it with his eyes.

"You can come back later to check on her," Don Francisco said. He gripped his staff and pushed himself up to stand. "I have food at home that the baby's family gave me. Take my bag and go build us a fire. We'll eat together. That is if you can separate yourself from my granddaughter."

Juan ignored her father's stare and squeezed Rosa's hand. He picked up the shaman's bag and headed toward the door. Rosa's mother put her hand on his face. "Thank you," she said.

Doña Mariana put a knobby hand against his chest and nodded enthusiastically. "Well done, Juanito, well done," she said. He couldn't help but smile at the old woman. Her divergent eyes radiated such approval.

"How is Alicia?" he asked. "Has she had her baby?"

The old woman shook her head. "She had false labor pains. I would have been here sooner, but her mother insisted that Alicia was about to deliver."

Juan pulled the door shut behind him. The family's old black dog wagged its tail. Its snout pointed toward the sky. It was a new moon. The Eyes of the Jaguar stared down, its celestial body hidden in inky blackness. The four stars of the Southern Cross held the corners of the universe in perfect alignment. Constellations clustered around the Milky Way. With a loud whoop, he ran down the road to tell his parents about Rosa. Then he would go to Don Francisco's house. He swung the bag by his side and whistled the melody of the shaman's flute loud enough for all the stars to hear. He laughed when he heard the dog howl back, its soulful cry fading into the stillness of the perfectly dark night.

Chapter Sixteen

After the third serving of corn chowder, Juan's belly was round and hard. He belched and wiped his sleeve across his mouth. He set his bowl down and slid back onto the wooden bench next to Don Francisco. The shaman glanced up from the fire with his eyebrows arched. "You're not finished already, are you?" he said.

"It was good," Juan said.

Don Francisco pulled the blanket up to his chin. He tamped a pinch of tobacco with his thumb into a well-worn pipe. Juan held a stick from the fire over the bowl until he heard the tobacco crackle. "While your food's settling, why don't you go bring in more firewood?" said the shaman. "Lately it seems that the cold comes into my bones to spend the night."

The eucalyptus wood, already split, was easy to stack against the oven. The green wood burned hot. Orange sparks popped out and had to be brushed off the rug on the floor. Don Francisco patted the bench next to him. "Come and keep an old man company," he said.

Juan sat and stretched out his legs. How did the shaman do it? Was it the *q'uyas* and the flute he played that brought Rosa back to life? That crystal heart was pulsing with light. And there was the staff, the *agua de florida*, the tobacco smoke, and the condor feather. Don Francisco might have had a magic potion in his mouth when he healed the wound on her head. But it was the song that finally awakened her.

Don Francisco broke the silence. "What is it you want to know?" he asked.

"I want to understand how you saved Rosa," Juan said. "Could you teach me how to do this work?"

The old man drew deeply on his pipe. "I did," he said. "At least, all that I can. The rest is up to you."

"But I can't do what you did. I need you to show me how to heal like that," Juan said.

"Who taught you how to crawl, how to walk?"

Juan started to speak but stopped when he caught the gist of the question. "I just learned, I guess."

"You taught yourself by trying different ways to do what you had to do, what you were called to do by the very necessity of life. And that's not so different from how I learned to do what I do," Don Francisco said. His chest shook with a paroxysm of coughing, darkening his face with the effort. Juan grabbed the kettle from the oven and added the fresh-brewed coca tea to the shaman's cup. Don Francisco sipped it until his cough settled. "Of course, it's helpful to have a good teacher when you're first learning," he said.

"That's what I mean," said Juan. "I want you to teach me."

The old man set his pipe down on the hearth and rubbed his face. He stared into the fire. The branches had broken into chunks of red and orange embers when he finally answered. "Juanito, you remind me of another young man. He, too, was eager to learn. I'd hoped that he would teach the next generation of healers for our people, but..." Don Francisco broke into another fit of coughing before he could finish. He took a swallow of tea and pulled the blanket around his shoulders. "I am old, and there's much for you to learn. Whether there's enough time is the question."

"But you told Rosa and me..." Juan said.

The shaman's eyes sparked. "I remember what I said. It's been my dream that there would be others who could carry the wisdom of the ancient ones into the next generation. Who else will teach our traditions to the child that we baptized today? She stands on our shoulders. We must be mindful of that trust." He touched his finger to Juan's chest.

"The missionaries spoke of illness as something that came into a person's experience from the outside," he said. "It was 'the stain of original sin' given to them for their disobedience by a judging God. This is similar to what sorcerers believe, except they claim it is an evil spirit or a curse from an enemy that causes a person to be sick. The doctor in Paucartambo scoffs at the sorcerer. He says that 'disease' is what sickens people and believes that this is more advanced. But I think that there is still a better way to look at this."

"How?" asked Juan.

"The healing traditions of our people are based in nature, and nature is based on *ayni*," he said. "That which we offer matches that which we attract into our experience. I believe that the root of health grows from inside of a person. Hopelessness, fear, or anger create imbalance in a person. Any one of these has its own set of circumstances that can manifest in disease or accidents. Do you understand?" Juan nodded.

"When someone comes to me with an illness, I look beneath their fear and confusion to find out who they really are," he said. "'Where is their heart?' I ask myself. What is their dream, the one that fills them with passion? Every person needs to believe that there is a way to get to where they want to go. But they must understand that only they can walk this path, and that it's an inside journey. The thoughts that they think will either help or hinder them on the way to their destination. It's true about wellness or anything else that they desire. This is only my opinion, but I believe that it is a good one. Do you understand?"

"Some, but not all of it," Juan said. "You called Rosa back into her body. I saw it with my own eyes, but I can't explain it. That's why I need you to show me. Teach me what I need to know."

The old man remained silent. His eyes disappeared behind fluttering lids that left only yellowed sclera exposed. The shaman had to be looking into the upper world. When he spoke, his voice sounded distant and his tone was oddly flat.

"What are you looking for?" he said. "You've never said why you want to become a healer. Is it just to learn how to do magic? Maybe it is the good opinions of others that you want. You think that the respect of others will make you worthy again. But why feel unworthy? This is what keeps your happiness buried inside. What is it that you really want?"

Juan didn't know how to respond. He wanted to be a healer like him. The shaman had called it the path of the jaguar. But if he decided to follow that path, where would it take him? It was the old man, the one who wore the jaguar claws, who knew the answer.

"That's it, isn't it," said Don Francisco. "It's Otorongo that brings you here. You are intrigued by its power, and you have many questions about this teacher of death. Yet there was great fear in your heart when you saw Rosa lying there cold and lifeless. You wanted to run, just like you did on the day that Marta died. You want forgiveness for your sister's death, but you are afraid that you are unworthy of forgiveness. This is what keeps you trapped," he said. "Until you stop blaming yourself, you will always be afraid to live fully from your heart. Otorongo can teach you about death, but such a lesson comes with great risk. To have a direct experience with this jaguar is one of the greatest dangers that a shaman can face."

His words cut deeper than the claws hanging around his neck could have. Even though the shaman had been able to save Rosa, his sister's death would always be his fault. The old man said that he shouldn't blame himself, but Juan doubted that even he could suck that wound out. It was buried too deep. And what did he mean about a 'direct experience'? He'd already had enough of those with the black jaguar.

The wind picked up and cold air snuck through the cracks around the door. Don Francisco pulled the blanket over Juan's shoulders. When the shaman spoke, it was with a casual tone that suggested their conversation was an ordinary one, one that men might have from time to time.

"You were but a boy then, and no one could outrun a storm like that," he said. "What happened to your sister wasn't your fault. But her death will haunt you the rest of your life, if you don't find a way to make peace with it. You have to find a way to shed the skins of your past. Only then can you find out who you really are and what it is that you want." He pulled thoughtfully on his pipe. "I think that your sister comes to you at night for a reason. She is trying to show you something important."

Juan stared at Don Francisco. The old man had seen the bad dream. No matter how hard he tried, he would never be able to leave that nightmare behind. The shaman blew another plume of smoke out.

"I've been walking this path for almost sixty years," he said. "I've learned that fear can be a treacherous enemy that plays tricks on you, or it can be a trusted friend that warns you at the right time. A healthy sense of fear is essential for survival. But when it comes from outside the present moment, you have made it an enemy. Until you deal with that day with Marta, you will always be at its mercy."

"But I can't change what happened that day," Juan said.

"To be a shaman is to know how you create your own reality. But such knowledge does not come easy, nor does it come in a single night."

"Why can't you help me, Don Francisco? I'll do whatever it takes," said Juan.

"To follow Otorongo's path with awareness takes years of practice. I traveled far and wide when I was a young man, and I studied with many teachers to learn what I know. Most have since crossed over to the world of Spirit. There are a few left like Doña Mariana and myself who still work in the way of the ancestors. But neither of us has enough time left to teach you how to become a shaman."

"There has to be a way. Just tell me what to do."

Don Francisco pursed his lips and studied Juan's face. He nodded. "Perhaps there is a way. It may be the only way. The challenges are substantial, and the risk is great. I don't know…"

"Just tell me," Juan said.

"It would be dangerous, and there is little time to prepare. And you would have to go alone."

"Where would I go?"

"To the Snow Star that sits at the top of Apu Ausangate," Don Francisco said.

Juan stared in disbelief. Of course the path of the jaguar led to that mountain. He had swallowed the hook that lay hidden in the old man's words. And the opaque eyes intimated that it was too late to spit it out. The shaman wanted him to follow the footsteps of his father on a pilgrimage that had almost cost him his life. Juan leaned over and buried his face in his hands. Instead of finding a way to leave Marta's death behind him, he had been challenged to face his own.

Don Francisco threw more wood on the fire.

Chapter Seventeen

The family of torrent ducks veered around Juan and floated downstream. With his pant legs rolled up, it felt good to stand in the cold current of the Puma Rimac. His muscles ached from the long hours harvesting potatoes. He had scrubbed the last of the black dirt from his hands when he heard Rosa call his name. He waded back to shore and put his sandals on. Doña Mariana must have taken off the poultice this morning. It had been three days since the accident.

Rosa grabbed his arm, and he helped her down onto the path along the river. She kissed him on the cheek. He had seen her after he had finished work yesterday, but it had been hard to talk with her parents there.

"How do you feel?" he asked.

"The swelling and the redness are gone, but I am still unsteady on my feet," she said. "My grandfather said that the injury to my head affected my balance. He said that it will get better with time. My father worries too much. My accident really scared him, but I'm okay." She lifted her bangs and showed him the scar. Juan winced when she grabbed his finger and touched it to her forehead. "There's no pain at all," she said. "My grandfather said that I should tell you what happened to me at the dance."

He would rather talk about their new land or anything else besides that. Rosa glanced at him and hesitated. "I'm listening," he said.

She took his hand. "I saw your face after I had fallen. You were scared. I wondered why there were so many people crowded around us. I got back up to dance, but you were still on your knees. I called to you, but you didn't hear me."

Juan stopped and looked at her. Her eyes had that faraway look.

"A roaring wind caught me like I was a piece of straw," she said. "The next thing I knew, I was between two huge rocks, standing over a channel of water. People with hair down to their waists circled around me. They held out their hands. They wanted me to come with them. Their faces were filled with too much light for me to see who they were."

It was too strange to be coincidence. He had seen those people when he had prayed for her that night and during the plant ceremony with her grandfather.

"I know it sounds crazy, but that's what I saw," she said. "Then a jaguar leapt in front of me. It was black, just like the one we saw. I was scared and didn't know what to do. That's when I heard a sound."

Juan stared at her. "A sound?" he said.

"It was sort of a whistle that came from a distance, but it grew louder. It got dark again, and the wind blew even harder. I was spinning through a tunnel and..." Rosa scrunched her eyebrows together and rubbed her forehead.

"Then what?"

"I landed on my back. It was too dark to see anything, and I was so cold. Then I felt a warm tingling spread through my body. I wondered if I had crossed over to the Spirit world. When I opened my eyes, I saw my grandfather and you looking at me like I had."

"I was scared that I had lost you forever," Juan said. "I knew what happened was my fault. I keep thinking about what I did wrong. Your grandfather said that nothing happens by accident. Fear or anger create imbalance in a person, he said. Maybe I really am cursed because of what happened to Marta. You might always be in danger because of me."

A look of uncertainty clouded Rosa's face, and she looked away. "Don't be silly. Besides, there is more to it than that," she said. "My father told me on the morning of the festival that he had heard rumors about us. He tried to convince me to dance with Pepe. He said that he was a stable young man from a good family. I told him that I wasn't going to dance with anyone but you. I was so angry that I could hardly speak. If anyone was out of sorts, it was me."

Rosa avoided his eyes and watched the ducks push their ducklings onto the bank. The light from the setting sun made her skin honey-like. *Open your eyes to yourself and see the light that shines there,* he heard. A flash of green feathers darted over his head. "What did you say?" he asked.

"I didn't say anything," she said. "Are you okay?" She felt his forehead. "You look tired. You haven't said much. You never told me what you talked about with my grandfather the other night."

Juan kept his eyes fixed on the path ahead. He wasn't sure what to say. Don Francisco had acted hurt when he told him that he wasn't sure about the journey to the mountain and that he needed time to think it over.

"To tell you the truth, the last few days have been a welcome break," he said. "Even though my father still tries to get me to work faster, things are better between us. Just today, he asked me how I wanted to plant my fields for next season."

Rosa stopped and waited until he looked at her. "And what did you tell my grandfather?"

He shouldn't have been surprised. She already knew what Don Francisco had asked him. "I've got until tonight to decide if I'm going to Ausangate."

"It's true what I told you," she said. "I was mad at my father that morning of the festival. But it wasn't about the dance. It was about going to the mountain. Juanito, this has been always been my dream. Ever since Marta told us those stories about our ancestors at the top of the sacred mountain, I've wanted to go. We promised each other that we would go someday. I told my mother that the day was soon coming when you and I would take this journey together. My father was furious when he found out, and he forbade me to ever speak of it again. I didn't say anything, but I was going when you were ready."

"But you know how dangerous that trip would be?" Juan said.

"I know," she said. My grandfather said that with what happened to my head, the risk would be too great in the higher altitudes. It will take time for my balance to come back. He said that you would have to go for both of us."

"But what kind of chance would I have? My father had studied with Don Francisco for almost three years, and he almost died on that mountain. That's not all. Your grandfather said that Marta comes in dreamtime to show me something important. But my father says that some things are best left alone. Maybe he's right, and I would be happier just farming. I could build a good future for us." She took her hands from his arm. He saw disappointment in her eyes.

"Why are you afraid?" Rosa said. "You've traveled in the mountains before, and you're strong."

A flash of green feathers caught Juan's eye. It was a hummingbird, like the one he and his mother had seen. He watched it disappear into the tall grass along the river. "It's not that I can't do it," he said. "But there is more to it than just hiking up a mountain." The purple-tinged green bird flew at his head. Juan held up his arm and ducked. "That crazy bird is attacking me," he said. "Let's go. Your father will be mad if you're not home before dark." Rosa tucked her arm into his. The hummingbird hovered for a moment before it darted off after an insect.

When they stood in front of her house, she looked at Juan. "My grandfather's health isn't the best. He said that you would have to go while he could still help. Otherwise the chance for you to carry his knowledge into the next generation might be lost forever. Maybe going to the Snow Star is a crazy idea. But what if you could meet our ancestors and learn to heal in the ancient ways? Wouldn't you want to at least try? If you do, then talk to my grandfather before it's too late. Let him help you."

He watched the clouds over Ausangate's peak catch the light of the setting sun. The night he worked with Don Francisco was beyond anything that he could have imagined. What if he could heal others in the way the shaman had?

They stopped in front of the doorway of Rosa's house. He put his finger on the corner of her mouth that hung down and pushed it up. "Maybe your grandfather could help me see a way," he said. She put her hands around his neck and pressed her lips to his. Her mouth tasted like *muña*. The sound of footsteps along the rocky path interrupted them. It was Rosa's grandfather. He walked past without any indication that he saw them. Juan glanced at Rosa.

"Go talk to him," she said. "It's important that he hears this tonight." She pushed him toward the path.

"Don Francisco, wait," he said. "I need to talk with you." The shaman grunted, but he kept walking toward his house. When they arrived at the front door, he turned toward Juan. His droopy eyelids covered half his eyes.

"What do you want?" he said.

Juan wanted to tell him that it had always been his dream to follow the shaman's path. He had known it since he was a boy and he and Rosa pretended to be the ancestors. When his sister died, he thought his dream had died with her. He knew he had to put Marta's death behind him. But the shaman wasn't interested in his words. It was his heart that he wanted to know about. He could only hope that he measured up to what lay ahead.

"Do you think that I could find the way to the Snow Star?" he asked.

"Rosa and I have to prepare more San Pedro tea," Don Francisco said. "Come back the day after tomorrow." He looked back before he stepped inside the house. "And bring your father with you."

Chapter Eighteen

The news about Rosa and how her grandfather had performed a miracle spread quickly through San Mateo. Men stopped his father in the fields and said that it was good that the shaman had taken Juan under his wing. The old man wouldn't be around forever, they said, nodding sagely. Juan studied Humberto's face for clues, but it was an impenetrable mask. He waited until the end of the day, when the other men were leaving the fields, to ask his father about Don Francisco's request.

"Papá..." he said. Humberto laid his hand on Juan's shoulder. A mixture of sadness and pride filled his father's eyes.

"I've seen it in your face all day," Humberto said. "I suppose your heart is set on the shaman's *hatun karpay*. It doesn't surprise me that the old man talked you into a journey of initiation to Ausangate. It was just a matter of time, I guess."

Juan was surprised, but his father must have known this day would come. He too had once heard the call of the sacred mountain.

"Don Francisco said that he wanted to see you," Juan said.

Humberto's face darkened and his knuckles tightened around his hoe. He studied the distant peaks of Ausangate before he looked back at Juan. "If this is what you want, I'll talk with him," he said.

"Can we go tonight?"

Humberto looked toward the village and nodded. They walked in silence to the shaman's house, their hoes slung over their shoulders.

Pacing back and forth outside, Juan heard the voices rise inside the house, but he couldn't make out what either man said. The shaman would know if he were close enough to listen in on their conversation. When Humberto stepped out, his face was

111

grim. "Go inside," he said. "He's waiting for you. You'll spend the next three days with him. Listen to everything he says. Ask questions when you don't understand. What you learn from him could save your life." He took the hoe from Juan's hand. "I'll be gone for a couple of days," his father said. "I have some business to take care of. I will see you when I get back." Humberto left with the burros the next day.

That night Juan and Rosa worked in ceremony with Don Francisco, and the following morning the shaman taught. In the afternoon Juan and Rosa took a walk along the river and shared their experience with the plant medicine. Each of the following days began early and lasted well into the evening. And with each ceremony Juan learned to see more of the light energy that Don Francisco talked about. The last day Rosa took Juan to visit Doña Mariana. The old medicine woman showed him the proper way to make a *despacho*. She pulled out tiny paper-wrapped bundles of seeds, sweets, play money, llama fat, and a thumb-sized llama to make an offering for his journey and for the people of San Mateo. "Offer your gift to the mountains and to Pachamama from your heart," she said. "Let the *apus* and Mother Earth know how much you appreciate them, and they will bless you and our village. Our crops will be good, our herds will grow, and we will prosper. This is *ayni*." He and Rosa burned the *despacho* on a hill that overlooked the village. The smoke would carry their prayers to the mountains, Rosa said. Juan spent the last night at home.

The whole family was up early the next morning. Juan waited by the fire, packed and ready to go. He touched his mother's shoulder when she had finished dressing his sisters. Her cheeks, smudged with soot, were marked by wet streaks. She handed off the youngest girl to José and wrapped Juan in a fierce hug. Her voice vibrated against his chest. "From my womb to my arms and from my arms to the earth, you've learned to stand on your own two feet. And now you must find your own way."

He swallowed the tightness in his throat and waited for his mother's eyes to focus on his lips. "Don't worry," Juan said. "I'll be okay." She tied the strings of his hat underneath his chin.

José pretended to untie them. Juan hooked one arm around his brother's neck and pulled his sisters toward him with the other.

"Take care of the herd," he told José. "And try to keep these girls out of trouble while I'm gone."

His father put his hand to the door. "We need to go. Don Francisco will be waiting," he said.

The stars along the faint edge of daybreak had disappeared when Juan and his father left the house. They walked in awkward silence through the village. Juan looked to the snow-capped mountains in the east. Shifting reds tinted the overhanging clouds. Sunlight had yet to spill out over the glaciers. He thought about Marta. She'd promised to take him and Rosa to Ausangate.

His father also gazed at the distant peaks, the furrow deep between his eyebrows. "I trust that Don Francisco has prepared you for the challenges ahead," Humberto said. Juan's father had told him very little about what to expect. The shaman had insisted on Humberto's silence before he had agreed to help.

"We worked with San Pedro," Juan said. "Don Francisco said that the plant would help me to perceive the spaces and the connections between things better. The mountain would teach me the rest, he said. I am sure he knows more than he's told me. But it's hard to get a straight answer from him. I hate it when he stares at me, and I don't have any idea what he's thinking."

Humberto's lips tightened into a thin smile. "You're not the only one who's had this experience with Don Francisco," he said. "Most of the men in San Mateo have felt the same when they've had dealings with your teacher. He can be intimidating."

"Like those claws around his neck," Juan said. "I asked Rosa, but she told me to ask her grandfather. How do you think he got them, Papá?"

"They are fierce-looking, indeed. They have been his since he was a young man. No one knows for sure, but there are lots of stories. One is that he had taken his family's herd to graze in the high pastures. He traveled farther and stayed longer than usual. It was a long distance from the village when the sun dropped behind the mountains. He was able to find a cave tucked in between several boulders."

"What happened?"

"He built a temporary corral of brush and stones for his animals, and he sat inside the cave to watch over them. Soon his chin rested on his chest. The hair on his scalp must have stood on end when he heard the coughing growl of a jaguar and felt its moist breath on the back of his neck. No one knows for sure what happened that night, but he came back the next day with the herd intact. His hair, black as a moonless night, had turned whiter than bones bleached by the sun."

"But the claws, Papá, how did he get the claws?"

"They were a gift, he said. People were afraid to ask him any more questions. You are not the first to feel his stare. They say that your teacher embodied the spirit of Otorongo that night."

Walking by his father's side, Juan remembered how the shaman described the jaguar. It was the teacher of death and it suffered fools not at all. Neither did his teacher. When he and Humberto reached Don Francisco's home, the sun was still hidden behind the crest of Ausangate. His father put a hand on his shoulder. "I'll wait for you here," he said.

Before he could knock on the sagging door, Juan heard the voice from inside.

"Come in," the shaman said. "I've been waiting for you."

He ducked under the low entrance, pushed the door shut, and set his gear down. He added several branches to the fire and lifted the kettle from the stones. He glanced at Don Francisco, but the old man waved him off. He poured a cup of tea and carried it outside to his father. When he came back, he took a seat on the wooden bench.

Don Francisco wore his hat decorated with scarlet feathers. When he opened up his *mesa* cloth, he picked up a white pouch with repeating patterns of stars woven into the alpaca. He blew the names of Apus Inkawari, Ausangate, Ocongate, and the other mountains of the Cordillera Vilcanota range onto the pouch before he placed it into Juan's hands. The pouch was heavy. He cupped Juan's hands inside his own.

"The legends say that before time existed, everything was one thing," he said. "Spirit lived in the empty space of timelessness,

the endlessness of all that is. But it wanted more, for Spirit also
has dreams. Faster and faster it swirled in an endless spiral when
a force so strong that it is impossible to imagine was unleashed.
Spirit spun its passion into all of creation and into each sentient
being. Mother Earth, Father Sun, Grandmother Moon, and all
the stars were born. The ancient ones called this dance
the *pachacuti*.

"And from this dance a piece of heaven fell on top of
Ausangate. It's called the Snow Star. It is where I received the
stone in this pouch, many years ago. When you reach this place,
leave this there. It will be your offering. Do you understand?"
Juan nodded. "Do not open the pouch until you are certain that
you are at the Snow Star," Don Francisco said.

"But how will I know when I have found it? What does it look
like?" Juan asked.

"This mountain has always watched over our people," the
shaman said. "From the beginning of time, medicine men and
women have made their pilgrimage to Ausangate to embody the
spirit of this mountain. They seek to become an *alto mesayoq*,
one who is not only a powerful healer but also a teacher. These
shamans can influence the weather and bring the rains after the
fields have been planted."

Juan started to speak, but Don Francisco's impatient look
silenced him.

"Spirit enters an *apu* through its snow star. That star is the
source of life for the mountain. Those who find it are able to
see from a perspective beyond ordinary time and space. They
receive the wisdom to become a *curak akullek*, a learned chewer of
coca leaves. Such shamans step between worlds to talk with the
ancient ones. They heal from great distances and can even use
earthquakes to create change."

"But where..." Juan said.

"The path to a snow star lies between that which can be
seen and that which remains unseen," Don Francisco said. "Ask
Ausangate to show you the way. The mountain will speak to
you within your own heart, if you will only listen. When you
reach the Snow Star, you will understand what I have told you

and much more than I can say." The shaman raised his shaggy eyebrows, and his bony fingers squeezed Juan's hands around the pouch. "Do you understand?" he said.

He had to trust Don Francisco. It was the only way he would make it to the Snow Star and come back alive. "I understand," he said.

"Make a *despacho* on your third night on the mountain," said Don Francisco. "The next day you will hike to the summit. Doña Mariana has taught you how to prepare this offering. Have you brought what you need?"

Juan nodded. It was all neatly bundled into separate packets inside his bag. Doña Mariana had given them to him last night.

"Good," Don Francisco said. "Mother Earth blesses us with that which we give to her. She will know that you understand *ayni.*" The shaman reached into his bag and handed Juan a bundle of coca leaves. "You have traveled with the men of the village deep into the jungle to harvest these. When you chew the leaves, remember the bounty of Pachamama and show to her your appreciation along the way. With each *k'intu,* ask her for guidance and for safe passage. You leave here as my apprentice. And when you return…we shall see."

Chapter Nineteen

A frail-looking man and two women with white braids that hung in front of their shoulders waited outside with Humberto, Doña Mariana, and Rosa. His father introduced Juan to the visitors. They were medicine people from neighboring villages, each with their own gift, he said. Juan wondered whether their loud conversations with Don Francisco were from excitement or from hearing that had diminished over the years.

When they had finished talking, the shaman rested his hand on Juan's shoulder. Humberto stood stiffly on the other side. The rest made a circle to the left and to the right of them. Doña Mariana swept her medicine bundle down the front and the back of each person. Rosa handed them a *k'intu* of coca leaves. When Juan tried to catch her eye, she looked away.

"We are here to send this young man on his journey of initiation to Apu Ausangate," Don Francisco said. "He seeks to be a healer in the lineage of our ancestors. We pray that he returns from the Snow Star with a vision for our people." The shaman handed him the rattle.

Juan called to the mountains of the Cordillera Vilcanota. He sang to Sachamama, serpent spirit of the south, to ask her guidance in the lower world. He summoned Otorongo, jaguar spirit of the west, to help him walk the shaman's path in the middle world. He called on Q'inti, hummingbird spirit of the north, to open his ears to the wisdom of the ancestors. He prayed to Hatun Kuntur, condor spirit of the east, that he might fly wingtip to wingtip with Spirit into the upper world. Then he put his hand on the ground.

"Pachamama, bone of our bone and Spirit of our Spirit, may we walk in harmony with all creation," he said. He pushed up off the ground and faced the east. "Inti Taita, bringer of day, let us feel your fire in our head, our heart, and our belly. Mamaquilla and Star Brothers and Sisters, shine your light to guide us through the seasons. Illa Tici Viracocha, Great Spirit, God of a thousand names and you who are the nameless one, may we hear you in the stillness of our hearts."

Juan took off his hat and bowed his head. Don Francisco's fingers were cold, but his breath felt warm against the top of his head. His prayer, murmured in tones that one might use with a child, was too faint to hear.

Each elder stepped forward and pressed a *q'uya* into Juan's hands. One was a piece of meteorite to clear headaches, another was a crystal to remove sadness from a broken heart, and the other was a llama carved of stone that was good for fertility. Doña Mariana gave him a shuttle made of polished bone. It was for weaving dreams, she said. He touched each *q'uya* to his lips before he tucked it into his bag.

The last person to come forward was his father. The dim light softened the scars on his cheeks. Juan saw a look in his eyes that he had forgotten. It was the father who pulled out tiny carved animals from his and Marta's ears. It was the father who told them stories when they were little, who held him on his lap. Humberto pressed the carved condor into his hands, the one that he had carried on his journey to Ausangate. "Your mother and I pray for your safe return," he said.

Humberto's eyebrows rose with surprise when Don Francisco held out his *mesa*. His father wrapped his hands around the medicine bundle of his old teacher, and they nodded in silent agreement. When Humberto touched Juan with the *mesa*, his prayer sounded more like humming than words. "I have not forgotten the light of my dream, for how could a father forget a son?" he sang. "Ausangate has called to my son, and the *apu* will teach him to sing. The sacred mountain said to send my son, and his song will be heard."

He pressed the bundle over Juan's head, his chest, and his belly. Then he spoke in a loud, clear voice. "Walk the path to the mountain with a good heart. And listen to your inside voice." With that, the ceremony was over.

Don Francisco asked Juan to wait so that he might walk with him to the river's edge. After he had hugged his father goodbye, he stood quietly off to the side. He twisted the cords that hung from his cap, crossed and uncrossed his arms. Rosa must be inside her grandfather's house. Only moments before, he had seen her with Doña Mariana. He jumped when strong arms wrapped around his waist from behind. Rosa's chest flattened against his back.

"Feel my heart," she said. "Remember this moment when you are at the Snow Star, because I will be there with you." When Juan saw her face, the red eyes told him that she had been crying. He wasn't sure whether it was because he was leaving or because she wasn't going with him.

"I made this for you," she said. He unfolded the cloth and held it up. Two eagles were woven into the dark blue alpaca weave. "It will be your *mesa* cloth, to hold the *q'uyas* that the elders gave you," she said. Before Juan could say anything, Rosa placed her finger across his lips.

He searched her face, taking in every detail. From the eyebrows that spanned her brow to the chipped tooth and to the funny way that one corner of her mouth dropped when she smiled, her eyes held it all together in a perfect balance. Rosa believed in him. He saw it in her face. He felt it in his heart. When he saw her again, he would ask her the question that he had asked when they were children. He brushed her cheek with his lips.

He bent over to gather his belongings. Rosa threw her arms around him when he came up to stand, knocking the bundle from his hands. He lifted her off her feet and squeezed her against his chest. She pressed her mouth against his ear. "I am with you always, light of my heart." From the corner of his eye, he caught Don Francisco's smile. The shaman headed down the trail toward the high pastures, his staff in hand. Juan kissed Rosa, grabbed his gear, and caught up with him.

He walked with the shaman along the edge of the village. He thought about the morning when he first saw the black jaguar. It was no accident, Rosa had said. It had come for him, his mother had told him. Don Francisco laid his hand on Juan's shoulder when they reached the river's ford. The eagle feather dangling from his teacher's hat brushed against his face. He followed the shaman's eyes to the crest of Ausangate.

"Our ancestors found ways of bringing the melting waters from glaciers over great distances through stone-lined channels to the fertile fields of the valleys below," Don Francisco said. "Pray that the spirit of the mountain flows through you like this. Align yourself with the energy of Ausangate. It is a powerful *apu.*" His face darkened with a harsh cough. Juan offered him a drink of water, but he waved him off.

"I have never been a patient person, and I've become even less so as the years of my life pass before me," the shaman said. "There has been such little time to prepare you for your journey of initiation. I know that I pushed you to take this journey. But if you are to be successful, you must trust your own knowing like you've never trusted it before. Listen to your inside voice. Trust what you feel, even if it feels crazy. Your heart must become your teacher. There is no other way. Do you understand?"

Juan was surprised. He had never seen Don Francisco this agitated before. The claw-like fingers dug into his shoulder with such urgency that he would have nodded yes just to release the pressure. "But there is something else that I need to tell you," he said. "It's about the reading of the leaves. There is more, more than I told your mother when I read them for her eighteen years ago." He dropped his hand from Juan's shoulder and studied the distant peaks. His eyes seemed to draw the mountains closer. And Juan did what he always did when he went inside another's story. He read their lips.

"Marta came to me with a question one day and said that I had to tell her the truth," Don Francisco said. "Always so many questions with that one." He smiled, but Juan saw the sadness in his eyes. "Your sister told me that Otorongo had called to her in dreamtime the night before. The jaguar was crouched inside a cave, and it told her to climb onto its back. It would carry her to where the ancestors lived, it said. But in her dream, I held her hand, and I told her not to go. Your sister asked me if I knew of such a cave." Don Francisco pursed his lips and pushed out a long breath. Juan didn't understand. What else hadn't he been told?

"She'd learned well how to read faces from your mother," Don Francisco said. "The way she looked at me, it was clear that she had figured out that I did know of such a cave. My heart sank to my stomach. I had seen her death in the coca leaves if she went there, but I could not hide from her the truth. I said that there was such a place, but I told her that Otorongo's power was too strong for a little girl. She had to be much older before it would be safe for her, I said. When Marta didn't say anything, I hoped that she had heeded my warning. But when I saw her body that day of the storm, I knew that she had found that cave."

It had to be the cave that he and his sister had sought on that day of storm. "Why did you wait until now to tell me this?" Juan said. "Did you think that I wouldn't go to Ausangate?"

"It was you who came to me," said Don Francisco. "You've been troubled about your sister's death ever since that day. That mountain is the only way that you'll find the peace you're looking for. Look at me," said the shaman. "When I read the leaves at your baptism, I saw that this way of life for our people would be changing, maybe not in my life but certainly in yours. Fewer and fewer would be content to live in the harshness of the *altiplano,* to plant and harvest potatoes and to herd animals back and forth to the high pastures. Rosa tells me that even now Alicia and her husband speak of moving to Paucartambo after their baby is born. They want more opportunity for their child, more than what is here in San Mateo. They want a better life for their family."

"I'm leaving on this journey to become a shaman for an *ayllu* with no future?"

"Our people have a future, but their lives will change when they leave our village for the cities. They know only how to farm, herd, and weave. They see an easier life in places like Paucartambo and Cusco. But they know nothing of what it's like to live alone among strangers in large towns and to find a job that will earn enough money for food and shelter. It's not easy to find work in those places when you don't know anyone. Men stand in line early each morning and hope to get hired for a few coins that day. Women sit on corners with their babies and try to sell their weavings to strangers so that they can buy enough food to feed their families at night. When their children are old enough, the parents will not be able to teach them. Nothing that they know will be important anymore. The children must go to school to have a future, but even that costs money."

"So what am I suppose to do?" said Juan.

"You can be a healer, but our people need more than that," said Don Francisco. "They need a vision that will guide them beyond the village. I know that Marta's death was hard on you and your family, and the memories from that day of the storm still haunt you. But you have to let the past go, like the serpent sheds her skin. Do you understand?"

Juan felt a familiar tightness in his throat. The bad feeling rose from his stomach. He looked back toward the village. Smoke wafted across the thatched roofs.

"There is no place to hide anymore. Step out onto the path ahead," the shaman said. "Your past will not help you. You've got to let your sister go. Do you understand?"

He didn't understand. Marta went to the cave despite Don Francisco's warning. She knew how dangerous it was. He and his sister should have never been anywhere near it. Juan knew that the shaman could see his anger. He couldn't help it. He was angry with his sister and he was angry with the shaman. His sister had known that death was waiting for her in that cave. And still she went. He should have been told. It wasn't fair. He had blamed himself all these years for what happened. The shaman's stare silenced him before he could open his mouth.

"There is something that I want you to do," Don Francisco said. "Choose a stone from along the trail and carry it with you to Pacchanta. The hot spring is near where the trail leaves the plateau and winds up into the foothills."

Marta had told him about this place where healers shed the skins of their past, but she had never told him about her dream.

"You'll know the right one to choose," the shaman said. "The stone will show itself to you. Give to it the pain of your past. It's been said that Sachamama bathes in the waters of Pacchanta.

Offer your stone there and call upon the serpent spirit to cleanse away that which no longer serves you. But don't linger too long. Sachamama is powerful and more than enough to overwhelm a young man," he said. The shaman's thin smile left Juan uncertain how to read his warning. Before he could ask, Don Francisco held up his hand.

"There's something that I want to give you," he said. He handed Juan the staff, reached underneath his poncho, and untied the leather cord from around his neck. There was a jaguar's claw in his left hand, but it was the scar that caught Juan's attention. It kept the shaman's ring finger in the shape of a condor's talon. Juan rubbed the same scar in his own left hand.

"Take this to Otorongo Q'ocha on the west side of the mountain," Don Francisco said. "Try to see your sister's death through the jaguar's eyes. I know you are angry with Marta and with me. Let go of your anger and disappointments and leave them with this claw in the jaguar lagoon. Ask for understanding about your sister's death and move on. I pray that you make peace with her. She was a beautiful girl and she loved you more than you know." Juan handed the shaman his staff back.

"No matter what happens, you must leave before the sun sets," Don Francisco said. "And then you will be ready to travel to the Snow Star." His eyes indicated that it was time for him to go. He rested his hands on Juan's shoulders and pressed his cracked lips against his cheek. "Your trip to Ausangate should take you three days, but your journey will last a lifetime," he said.

Chapter Twenty

Juan saw the smoke rising in the valley below and imagined José gathering the animals, his mouth full of potato. His father and the other men would be on their way to harvest barley from the yellow patches on the slopes of Inkawari. They would talk about the crops, the weather, and the upcoming festival for the La Virgen de Carmen in Paucartambo. The women left behind were in charge of the village. They did the cooking and the weaving, and they brought the children into the life of their community. That was the way it had always been, but for how much longer?

When he crested the top of the plateau, Juan stopped and scraped off a piece of *llipta* from a hard ball made of burnt quinoa, anis, and lime. He wrapped it in a wad of coca leaves and tucked it inside his cheek pouch. When he sucked the juice from the leaves, the *llipta* sweetened the taste of the coca. And it activated the coca, making it easier for him to breathe. The energy that the leaves provided would be valuable in the mountains that lay beyond the foothills.

Sunlight spread across the horizon and sharpened the edges of the distant white peaks. Humberto had told him that he needed to reach the hut on Ausangate before nightfall. Keep a good pace, his father said. It would be dangerous to try to trek up the mountain in the dark. The faint outline of the path meandered in serpentine fashion through the stiff grass. It cut across Puma Rimac several times, forcing Juan to roll up his pant legs and wade narrow stretches of icy water.

Scattered clouds passed like ancient masks across the face of the sun, covering the uneven terrain with a mosaic of shadows and light. Unmasked, the sun warmed the mountain air in moments, and Juan wiped the sweat from his forehead. When it slipped behind the clouds, the cold returned, and he slipped his arms underneath his poncho.

When a blur of iridescent green feathers brushed past him, he laughed in spite of himself and shook his finger at the hummingbird. The violet-masked bird stopped in front of his face, tilted its head to one side, and squeaked. "So it's you again. You are stalking me," he said. The bird flew ahead, darting from one *puna* plant to another. It landed on top of a thorny agave, looked back at him, and squeaked again.

The yellow *ichu* was thick against his legs by the time Juan reached the highest part of the open pasture land. He propped his hands on his thighs and studied the trail ahead. One branch switched back and forth along the edge of the foothills, following the river. The closer one cut its way through a rock-strewn incline topped by a clump of boulders. The hummingbird hovered by his head. "The trail straight up that knoll will save time," he said. The bird squeaked and flew ahead. Juan shifted the weight of the blanket around his shoulders and hastened his pace.

Halfway up the incline, he spotted a stone channel hidden in the *ichu*, flush with the surface of the ground. A trickle of water moistened the bottom. Juan followed the channel up the hill until he reached the boulders at the top. Gray slabs stood like silent sentinels, swallowing his silhouette with their shadows. Thick, woody vines with broad, dried leaves hung over a narrow crevice between two boulders. The stone channel disappeared into the cleft. He pulled the leafy canopy to the side.

A musty smell hung in the damp air, and dark walls glistened with an uneasy shifting light. Carved stones, nestled together with beveled seams, lined the sides. Don Francisco said that the highlands were once part of a vast civilization, even before the time of the Incas. This had to be one of the sacred sites of the ancestors. The shaman told him that such places would reveal themselves, if one was patient. There was much power in these places, he said. Juan ducked his head and stepped through the opening. Drops of water splashed into a simple round basin carved into the floor. Water spilled over the basin's edge into the channel.

An altar of solid granite with a seat carved into its base stood behind the basin. Pieces of crystal, figures carved of stone, and crumbling brown leaves dotted its surface. Juan laid three coca leaves on the altar, and he sprinkled it with *agua de florida*. With his gear off, he was able to tuck himself into the narrow seat. A steady drip echoed throughout the chamber. Drops from the slit of light in the ceiling landed in the dark pool below, forming circles insides circles. Pinpoints of light skittered across the pool. Juan leaned forward.

Ghost-like images of children floated in the water. His sister ran in front of him, her long legs widening the gap between them. Llamas and alpacas raced ahead. The cloven-footed animals scrambled around the rocks, their long necks waving in different directions. A thick, sour taste rose from Juan's stomach and burned his throat. It was the day of the storm, and this was the cave that they had sought to reach. He had to get out of here. His knees buckled when he tried to stand and he fainted, hitting his head against the stone basin.

Lightning crashed around him, and an acrid smell permeated the air. A heavy downdraft from the boiling black clouds blew sheets of water across the ground. His woolen cap blew off, but he couldn't stop. Hard raindrops stung his face and plastered his hair against his head. The sodden poncho hung heavy on him. He sought the faint path ahead, gasping for air. His heart was a fist pounding inside his chest. Sword-like leaves of *puna* plants whipped against his bare legs. Wet, heavy clay pulled on his sandals until they fell from his feet. The earth trembled before the next burst of lightning exploded in a thunderous crescendo. A sharp tingling in his feet made him jump up in the middle of a stride, but he was too scared to cry.

Marta came back for him, and she grabbed his wrist. She screamed, "The cave is our only chance." The strikes came closer, one on top of another. His sister pushed him ahead. "Run, Juanito, run," she said. The rest of her words were lost in the next crack of lightning. A wave of blue light surged past, lifting him off his feet. Low-lying clouds jerked him up into a funnel thick with water. He flailed against the invisible grasp that held onto him, fighting to breathe in the rain-laden air. His scream was lost in the roar of the wind. Another bolt of lightning struck, and he fell back toward the earth. Slammed against the drenched ground, he bounced several times before landing face down in a shallow puddle.

Coughing and gagging, he pushed himself up. He was shaking and could barely stand, but he had to find Marta. She would take them home. He weaved through flickering light and shadows and darkness, shouting for his sister. He tripped and fell down and got up again. A burst of lightning outlined her body. He knelt beside her and shook her shoulder. Her face was pressed against the ground. "Wake up Marta," he shouted. "You have to take me home." He grabbed onto her sweater with both hands to turn her over. Her head rolled to the side, and he staggered backward. Dark eyes stared vacantly from a charred face that had seen too much light. Her face was a hideous mask that a dancer at a festival might wear. Blood trickled from the corner of her mouth.

Marta had said that the ancestors would take them home if they were lost. He had prayed hard, but they never came. He had left her out in the driving rain and hid between the boulders. If he could see his sister again, he would tell her how much he missed her. But that wasn't going to happen. She wasn't ever coming back. Don Francisco was right. He had to let her go.

With his cheek pressed against the cold floor, he probed underneath his wool cap. There was no blood on his fingers, but his head hurt plenty. He pushed himself up onto his hands and knees. The echo of a steady drip filled the cave. A thin sliver of light from the ceiling, curved in the shape of a crescent moon, flickered across the surface of the pool. Dark eyes, cat-like in intensity, blinked several times, surprised at their own reflection. Lips parted and wide teeth shimmered.

Clear in every detail, it was his dark red face that looked back at him. And underneath, at the bottom of the pool, was a stone. It was a smooth, oval black stone crisscrossed with white lines. Juan picked it up, held it to his lips, and blew. This was the stone that he would take to Pacchanta. He would take it where

Sachamama lay coiled in the belly of the lower world. It was where shamans went to shed the skins of their past.

He left a *k'intu* on the stone altar and walked outside into the white light of the morning sun. He wondered how long he had been in the cave. The shadows said not much, but it felt that a lifetime had passed. Perhaps it had. His time for reflection was cut short when the hummingbird dropped down in front of his face. It peered into his eyes, hovering for a moment before it flew up the path that led toward the mountain. He watched until the bird disappeared over the boulders. "Q'inti," he murmured. Someone he knew was looking through those eyes, someone close to him.

Chapter Twenty-One

When Juan saw the mist that hung above the foothills, he thought it strange that there was still ground fog this late in the morning. He scrambled up the loose footing along the narrow trail until it stopped at a jumbled cascade of rocks. Different sizes and shapes of carved white stones lay piled in a steep hill. Tendrils of green vines emerged between the rocks. He wedged his fingertips and toes into cracks, shifting from handhold to foothold, and climbed up. The hummingbird waited for him at the top. A serpentine path wound its way down the other side of the hill. The dampness made the rocks slippery and the footing treacherous. Q'inti chattered excitedly over his shoulder when he slid down the last few feet on his back.

The steamy mist was even thicker when he reached the bottom. Green trees draped with rope-like vines grew out of the surrounding stone. A triangular shaped boulder was etched with serpent-like lines. His father had shown him similar carvings in the foundation stones of a cathedral in Paucartambo. Adobe walls had been built by Spanish missionaries on top of the destroyed Inca temple, Humberto said.

Juan pushed his way through the vines and climbed over toppled walls until he found the hot spring. It was Pacchanta, an opening into the lower world. He slid the heavy blanket off his back and knelt down by the water. The smooth, oval black stone with white lines from the cave fit into his hand like an egg nestled inside its nest. "Sachamama, guardian spirit of the lower world, let your healing waters cleanse that which no longer serves me," he said. But he was reluctant to let the stone go. It held the memory of his sister and the pain that had been his for so long. Maybe he shouldn't get rid of it. The rock could be a powerful healing q'uya for his mesa. He ducked his head just in time to avoid the diving hummingbird.

With an eye on Q'inti, he pressed the rock to his lips. "You hold what has been a long journey for me," he said. "I return you to the *ukhupacha*." He flung the stone into the waters of Pacchanta. Don Francisco warned him to make his visit short, but he wasn't leaving until he enjoyed a good soak. He pulled off the rest of his clothes and lowered himself down into the lagoon. Never before had he felt so warm. He stuck his head underneath. Marta's story about the hot spring was true. Maybe the past held a different kind of power than what he had imagined.

With his wet hair tucked underneath the wool hat, he slipped his clothes back on and spread his blanket near the lagoon. He stretched out his aching muscles underneath the shady green canopy. Q'inti buzzed around his head, brushing Juan's face with its wings. He waved the bird away and pulled his cap down over his eyes. "Go away," he said. "You can be a pest." With hands folded across his chest, Juan's sonorous breathing soon drowned out the bird's protests.

The snake's yellow eyes and nose sat high on its huge triangular head. It stared at him, touching his cheek with its flickering tongue. Moist, yellow coils, covered with alternating pairs of black blotches, pinned his arms to his sides and locked his legs together. "Help me, Q'inti," he cried. The anaconda's pressure around his chest choked his plea to a hoarse whisper.

Speak, he heard. He prayed frantically for the hummingbird, but it was nowhere to be seen. *Speak to the snake*, the voice said. This was crazy. He had to wake up from this nightmare. The third time he heard the voice he spoke.

"Sachamama," he said. I came to your waters to heal my past. My stone from the cave lies deep within your waters, swallowed into the *ukhupacha*. Serpent spirit, speak and I will listen." But all he heard was the sound of his own breath. *Your breath, remember your breath*, the voice said. Juan forced himself to breathe slower and deeper. The snake's coils writhed around him. A tingling at the tip of Juan's tailbone moved upward along his spine. A wave pressed against the inside of his skull. The pressure pushed through his crown and a warm yellow light washed over him. The coils pulsed with the rhythm of the flow.

He wondered if the woman's voice was his imagination until he felt her tongue flick against his ear. "You've asked for my blessings," she hissed. "You want freedom from the pain of your sister's death. But you have always been free. It is you who bound yourself with guilt and shame and then worried about how others might judge you. The present is a gift that you give to yourself. All of your power lies in the present. It will never be found in your past. Why give yourself something that you do not wish to receive?

"You have felt the earth mother moving through you," she said. "The deep underbelly of the Pachamama is fertile beyond your wildest dreams. Deep within, she holds the seeds of the desires that you have sown. Don't dig them up to see if they have sprouted yet. Instead, content yourself with pulling out the weeds that slow their growth. You summon much from creation with your wanting, but you grow anxious and fearful when you doubt that any of it will ever come to pass. What are you afraid of? This is what you must answer to be truly free. It's your fear that you must face if you want to be a shaman for your people," hissed the serpent. The tip of her tongue flickered inside his ear, and his eyes snapped open.

Condensation from the overhanging foliage dripped on him. Juan wiped his ear with his sleeve and sat up. In the green water, he saw the purple spot on the chest of the hummingbird. The bird, suspended by vibrating wings, hung above his head. He looked up. "Q'inti, where were you?" he said. The hummingbird squeaked back at him. "I know what you told me," he said.

Q'inti darted over to inspect something tattered and brown entwined between the rocks along the water's edge. Juan jumped up and followed the bird. It was a snakeskin from a very large jungle snake. Next to it was a triangular yellow stone. With two indentations for eyes, it looked like the head of the anaconda. The rock still held the moist heat of the water. Ignoring Q'inti's chatter, Juan tucked it into his bag and laid three coca leaves next to the snakeskin.

"We can talk about this later," he said. "We should go now."

When he crested the top of the next hill, he looked down at the misty lagoon. Don Francisco could have said more about Pacchanta. Juan moved quickly along the path toward Ausangate. The shadows from passing clouds crossed the rocks like creatures from another world.

Chapter Twenty-Two

Q'inti hung in front of him, its beak touching his nose. When Juan reached out to stroke it with the tips of his fingers, the bird flew over his head and back out between his legs. He laughed and chased it for a few steps, but he gave up when the hummingbird raced ahead. The incline was steep and the footing tricky through the slick, gray shale.

A breeze rippled through the long-stemmed *ichu* along the banks of the stream. He slid the blanket, heavy with supplies, off his back. A rock on the edge of the bank caught his eye when he bent over to wash his face. It was a triangular stone with a greenish hue and quartz crystals. He rinsed it off and touched it to his lips. He listened to the water splash against the rocks. Words echoed in his head, spoken by someone else. *All is of Source. We are not separate from that which you are.* When he opened his eyes, Q'inti was perched on the top of a thorny *puna* plant. He watched his *k'intu* of leaves float downstream before he tucked the stone inside his bag.

The trail on other side of the water was even steeper. With the sun straight up, he knew that he had to pick up his pace. He pursed his lips and dug in with the edge of his sandals. The path was one switchback after another, marked by an occasional stack of rocks. His toes were battered, and his heart pounded by the time he had crested the top of the last foothill. Ausangate stood majestic, its white peaks glistening against the dark blue sky. A jagged chain of snow-capped mountains stretched out on either side. Ausangate looked close, but Juan guessed that he was no more than halfway there.

The path wound its way along a ridge before it ended at an odd-shaped boulder. When Juan reached the front of it, he saw that the rock was twice his height and easily three times his width.

He went to walk around it, but the stone blocked his way. The higher elevation must be affecting him, he thought. He went around to the other side. Still he could not get around it. He pretended to turn around and then tried to run around the rock. He ran from side to side, but he could not get past.

Q'inti perched on top and fluttered its wings. Juan studied the top of the boulder. Its outline was identical to the crest of Ausangate. Don Francisco had said nothing about this. He reached into his bag and held up the triangular green stone from the stream. Water, wind, and time had worn it into the same shape as the rock. This had to be the key. He leaned it against the boulder and placed his hands and his head against the pitted granite surface. He closed his eyes and prayed. "*Huaca*, I follow the shaman's path to Ausangate. Allow me to travel to the home of my ancestors." He waited for a voice but heard only the gusts of the afternoon winds. *Maybe I should make an offering of coca leaves*, he thought. But he couldn't reach inside his bag. His head and his hands were stuck to the boulder.

The pounding of a hundred *wankaras* echoed inside his head, and the drums beat faster than any musicians could play. The ground opened in front of the boulder, and he slid on his back down a pitch-black crevasse. In only moments he stood in front of his family's home. The door hung open, but no one lived there anymore. A condor the size of a man soared toward him, and a thousand voices spoke at the same time. Juan tried to jump on the back of the huge bird, but it flew by him too fast. He spun downward into emptiness. He tried to shout to Q'inti, but the cry stuck inside his throat.

The woman sounded like a songbird when she spoke. "Follow the sound of my voice," she said. He was drawn into a tighter spiral until he landed with a firm thump. He opened one eye and then the other. Repeated v-shaped carvings of condors carved into the granite stretched between his hands. They were marks of the ancient ones. Don Francisco had said that there were many places that shamans traveled without walking. Underneath the sacred rock must be the opening to a world that he wasn't ready for yet. But whose voice had guided him back?

She sounded familiar, but he didn't know anyone who talked like that. When he looked down for his stone, it was gone.

He left a *k'intu* of coca leaves, tiptoed around the rock, and stepped back onto the trail. By the time he reached the base of Ausangate, the sun tilted toward the west. The growling in his stomach insisted that he take a break for lunch, but it would have to be quick. The distant gray clouds could reach the mountain by nightfall. Juan found a spot on a ledge that overlooked the *altiplano* to eat a handful of thumb-sized, light-skinned potatoes. Q'inti landed on his hand and picked out several morsels. When it finished eating, it hopped up to his shoulder and stretched out its wings.

Juan's eardrums vibrated with the buzzing sound. The drone of the hummingbird's wings grew louder until particles of sunlight scurried through the air like tuco-tucos, darting one way and then the other. Juan stared into the spaces between the jittery dots of light. The light became like snowflakes driven by a strong wind. He softened his eyes, and the light changed into shimmering lines that swept across a dark blue background. The lines folded and unfolded around him in graceful curves. The light danced to music played by an invisible flute. He saw and felt the rhythm of the notes, and he floated in the pauses. Waves of light washed over the shadowy rocks and boulders below. His eyes wavered until he succumbed to the vastness of it all.

Two condors soared across a dark blue tapestry. A dimly lit room crowded with plants filled with smoke. A raspy, guttural voice shouted into his ear, "You must go back. You cannot stay here." Startled, Juan sat up and looked around. Uneven layers of rock crested and dipped across the foothills below. The peaks of Ausangate towered above him. He had been in Don Francisco's home. The shaman had even yelled at him. Juan dropped his face into his hands.

He felt the tips of Q'inti's feathers brush against his face. The hummingbird perched on his hand. When he peeked through his fingers, unblinking dark eyes buttressed by iridescent purple feathers peered into his face. The hummingbird's gaze invited trust and spoke of an intimacy born from deep insight into his confusion. He felt a connection with the bird that stretched beyond his ability to understand. It had shown him a glimpse into another world. Or maybe it was a different way to see this one. Maybe this was what Don Francisco meant when he said that shamans look into the spaces between things and see a different reality. Q'inti rose up, its body suspended by an invisible thread. Its wings were but a shimmering vibration when it flew up the trail.

Chapter Twenty-Three

Gritty dust pelted his face, and his head pulsed relentlessly. His calves and thighs ached and began to cramp in the cold air. His feet, once sore, had grown numb from the long hours on the trail. One switchback became another. Half-buried rocks took their toll on his battered toes. His heart bounced against his chest. The thinner air turned breathing into hard work. With less pressure in the atmosphere to push air into his lungs, he had to rest more with his hands propped on his knees. He shortened his steps up the steep path. Even breathing through his nose parched his throat. An occasional sip of water helped, but his father had told him not to drink much water in the mountains. The cold liquid would sap his body heat, he said. Juan wrapped fresh leaves around a pinch of *llipta* and tucked the wad of coca into his cheek.

The waxing and waning wind picked up strength in the late afternoon when the sun touched the western peaks. Heavy gusts cut across the face of the mountain, alternating between sharp whistles and low fluttering moans. When dark clouds covered the top of Ausangate, flurries of ice pellets stung his cheeks. He tied the cords of his cap and stuck his hands underneath his armpits. It was the hour of power. The wind grew stronger late in the day so that it could blow out the sun and the earth could go to bed, his father had told him and Marta when they were children. He imagined his family gathered for dinner, his mother ladling out warm quinoa soup into a bowl with a potato in the middle.

But his home was at the end of this trail, at least for the next three days. Don Francisco had told him about a stone hut near Azul Q'ocha. The hut lay nestled on a tundra-covered plateau next to this blue lagoon. Used by travelers for longer than anyone could remember, it had been built to shelter those who came to talk to the mountain, the shaman said.

The hummingbird was nowhere to be seen. Maybe it had flown back down. It was too late for him to turn back. Cold, hunger, and cramping muscles were draining his reserves. He had begun to cough and needed to stop and rest. But to risk falling asleep in the open would be dangerous. Exhaustion, when the temperature dropped at night, could be fatal even for the hardiest of highland people. The trail, a scant foot wide in places, would be too treacherous to walk in the dark. He stuffed more coca leaves into his mouth. He had to find the hut.

It was twilight when the path widened into a flat open space bordered by clumps of rocks. The ground was spongy under his feet. Wind swept across the tundra, whistling with the high vibrato pitch of panpipes. Ice pellets turned into snowflakes. Clouds slipping down the mountain's peaks made it almost certain there would be no stars tonight. Juan squatted on his heels and buried his hands under his poncho. His head would burst if he didn't stop to rest. With his back to the wind, he closed his eyes.

He swatted at the incessant buzzing in his ear, but the noise persisted. *Your song,* said the voice. But Juan needed more rest. It was too cold to move, and he was too tired. He drifted back into a mindless exhaustion. The high-pitched squeak in his ear startled him. He peeked out of one eye. Q'inti's wings vibrated in a frenzied blur. The voice spoke louder. *Your song,* it said. It was no good to fall asleep now. He had to stand.

Juan shook his head. Gusts of wind tugged at his poncho when he stood up. The cold cut through his clothes with a sharp edge. The coca leaves flew from his hand, and his prayer was lost in the shrieking wind. He heard a wail of ghostly voices, shouting their warnings. Either his mind played tricks on him, or this was the work of vengeful spirits. The voice in his ear shouted. *Your song,* it said.

His *icaro* was halting and rough. "Ausangate, let me hear the voices of the ancestors in the wind," he sang. "I came to hear their songs. May my heart hear their words. Hey, hey, it is good to hear their songs." He sang the words again. He sang until the winds died down and the snow tapered to an occasional flake. He almost missed the hummingbird in the dim light when it darted across the open field and landed on a pile of stones. The faint outline of a thatched roof rose above the rock.

The stone walls of the circular hut were built around a natural rock outcrop. It took both hands to open the wooden door. Juan ducked underneath the doorway and dropped his gear. The room was small, but it was dry. Inside an alcove built against the opposite wall was a stone-lined pit. Sticks of eucalyptus wood leaned into a circle around a mound of twigs and dried grass. He struck the flint against a piece of metal until enough sparks fell onto the dry tinder and he saw a thin wisp of smoke. When the fire got hot enough to burn the wood, he warmed his hands until the numbness in his fingers became a painful tingling. He stepped back from the flames and looked around his new home.

Split wood was stacked against the wall. Cut grass for bedding lay on the other side of the room, and a bag of potatoes hung from one of the narrow poles that spanned the ceiling of the hut. Juan's eyes watered and a knot lodged in his throat. He remembered the exhaustion in his father's face after he had come back home last night. The burros had empty packs on their backs. He knew where Humberto had left the potatoes and wood. And he knew what it had taken for his father to have come here.

From the doorway he saw the night sky open. Cracks of inky black speckled with stars peeked through the cloud cover. The wind faded to a breeze that caressed his face with a feather-like touch. Only water splashing against rocks broke the stillness. Juan pulled the door behind him and followed the path down to the lagoon. A fish slapped its tail against the surface of the water before it disappeared back into the dark. Azul Q'ocha was a good place to find trout, Don Francisco had said. Juan took out a string with two sharp hooks tied to the end and threaded a kernel of corn onto each one. He swung the weighted cord over his head, casting it into the lagoon with a flick of his wrist. The other end he tied to a bush near the water's edge.

The cloud cover split open, and stars crowded the night sky. The Milky Way stretched across the heavens, and the Southern Cross pointed to the four directions. Two shooting stars crossed in the periphery of his vision. The Eyes of the Jaguar stared down at him. The jaguar's lagoon was the gateway to the middle world, the shaman had said. It was the world of the *kaypacha* where life and death danced together, and it was Otorongo who called the tune.

Don Francisco promised that his questions about Marta would be answered at Otorongo Q'ocha. He was to leave the claw at the lagoon. But at least he didn't have to worry about a real jaguar. One might wander from the jungle onto the *altiplano* but never to a glacier-covered mountain. That he was sure about. With his hands tucked under his poncho, Juan walked back up the path to the hut.

Chapter Twenty-Four

Only the cracks around the door kept the air fit to breathe in the cramped, smoke-filled room. Juan was too hungry and tired to wait any longer to eat. He teased out a handful of the thumb-sized potatoes from the pit. With his back against the wall and his feet next to the fire, he washed down the mostly cooked tubers with steaming cups of coca tea. The crackling flames of the eucalyptus made the place feel home-like. The cut grass and his wool blanket would make a good bed for a few nights on the mountain. In addition to the wood inside the hut, he could burn dried dung left from herds that grazed at the higher elevations.

The day had left him with many questions for Don Francisco. But even if the shaman had been inside the hut, Juan doubted whether he could keep his eyes open long enough to ask them. The cup fell from his hand before the fire had burned out. Sleep carried him to a place outside the walls of the stone hut.

The air was crisp with sunlight when he looked down on the glacier-capped mountains bordered by vast grasslands. Drawn to the tallest peak, he landed below the snow line near a heart-shaped cleft in the rock. Hidden in the shadows, a man waited at the entrance with folded arms. He wore only a simple white cloth around his waist. The sinewy muscles of his torso rippled cat-like when he turned toward the cave. "Come with me," he said. Something about the man's voice compelled him to follow.

With cautious steps, Juan passed through one turn and then another, descending deeper into the mountain. He followed the echo of footsteps until he wasn't sure whether the sound came from the man ahead or from his own steps. The silence startled him when he stopped to listen. One false move could send him tumbling inside the dark cavern. Afraid to go forward or backward, he froze. An invisible strap squeezed around his chest until he could hardly take a breath. Before he could shout for help, the stranger grabbed his wrists and slowly extended his arms until his fingers touched the cool, damp walls on either side.

Juan took a deep breath and stepped forward through the tunnel. With his fingertips brushing over the smooth rock, he felt his way through the curves of each turn. When he walked faster, the walls glowed with a dim light. The faster he walked, the brighter the narrow passageway became. He ran until his eyes watered and his forehead ached from too much light. He stopped and put his hands over his eyes. A wispy funnel spun from his brow and slipped through his fingers. His eyes stopped hurting and he dropped his hands. He stood inside a cavernous room. Light rushed around him in swirls and eddies.

He jumped when he heard the guttural voice behind him. It had to be Don Francisco. "You are finding another way to see," he said. Juan spun around. The man wore a string of claws around his neck, but his broad face did not have a single wrinkle. Black hair reached to his waist, and his eyes were dark as charred embers. The man's eyes twinkled, and the corners of his mouth played with a smile. "You are used to seeing the ordinary world," he said. "But this kind of sight is not with your physical eyes."

"What do you mean?" Juan said.

"When you were an infant, you used sight, touch, taste, smell, hearing, and movement to fill your world with meaningful pictures," he said. "Now you are learning to see through different eyes. This vision comes from inside of you. A shaman explores reality from a different perspective. He peers into the spaces between things to see the light that creates the physical world."

It made Juan uneasy to think that the ground beneath his feet was made out of light. It felt more secure to stand on dirt and rock. The light flickered, and the man's image grew dimmer.

"You must be willing to see beyond ordinary reality," said the stranger. "Learn how to create your own. Do you understand?"

"But how do I create this reality?" Juan said.

With his head tilted to one side, the man's lips parted with a smile. "It is not a puzzle for the mind to solve," he said. "You already create your own reality. But to be a shaman, you must learn to do it with awareness."

"How?"

The stranger sat on a white rock. Different colors of light fluttered around him when he spoke. "There are three parts," he said. "The first one is to know what it is you want. Life itself compels you to make choices about what you want. It happens whenever you desire something different than what you have."

"If I choose what I want, what's the next step?"

"The energy of Source flows like the waters of Puma Rimac to give you what you want in more ways than you can imagine. Ask and it is given. This is *ayni*. The clarity of your desire is what brings it to you."

"But don't I have to do something to make it happen?" said Juan.

"This part is the shaman's true work. It is to expect what you want will come. Learn to mold your thoughts into a strong belief. When your expectation matches the picture of what you want, your reality shifts. It is not nearly as hard as you imagine. A belief without self-doubt, worry, or contradiction will find its fulfillment in physical creation. That which is like unto itself is drawn. It is *ayni*. It must happen. A shaman who knows this stands on the leading edge of creation," said the man. "You already create your own reality, but it takes a clear head to do it with awareness."

Juan's head felt anything but clear. How could he believe what the man said? He hadn't asked the black jaguar to come to San Mateo. It didn't make sense. He remembered his mother's warning about the dangers of a sight disconnected from who he was. The flow of colors around the man slowed and melted into gray threads.

"Don't try to make sense of everything at once. If you know something too soon, you miss the deeper understanding. Choose a different thought if you don't like how that one looks," the man said.

"I don't understand."

"What feels better than fear and confusion?"

"If I knew how to play this stupid game, I would," Juan snapped. Vibrant red sparked around him.

"Anger felt better than fear and confusion, and it moved you toward more clarity," the man said. "You are back in focus and you feel better now, don't you?"

Juan had to admit that he was right. Iridescent blue swirled in front of his face.

"Think of your feelings as sounds made from the different instruments that musicians play at festivals," the stranger said. "Just as each instrument makes a distinct sound you can hear, each emotion has a unique signature that you can feel. Learn to dance to the rhythm of your feelings. There are many steps to go from fear or despair to a better feeling place. Great leaps are difficult, if not impossible, and rarely desirable. Trust your feelings when you have doubts or questions or when you have decisions to make. They are your connection to the energy of Source. Your joy, passion, and appreciation tell you when you are most in alignment with what you seek. Despair, sadness, anger, and frustration are also valuable. They let you know that you need to shift the focus of your attention to a thought that feels better, one that allows a more clear connection between you and the picture of what you want."

The man's words looked like butterflies dancing in the air. Juan thought about how it would be to create whatever he wanted. He imagined himself next to Rosa in the hot springs of Pacchanta. He saw the cinnamon brown color of her eyes and smelled the mint-like *muña* on her breath. He felt her arm press against his. Streams of iridescent light swirled around the room, encircling him and the man like strands of rainbow-colored yarn.

"You perceive more who you are now, my friend," his companion said. "But there is something else, something important that I want to give you about the nature of your Inner Being."

"My inner being?" asked Juan.

146

"Your greater, non-physical being, that which is an extension of *Illa Tici Viracocha,* Great Spirit, God of All That Is, the God of a thousand names and the one who is nameless. It is your eternal link to the pure, positive energy of Source."

"And how do I find this inner being?"

"By becoming more of who you are," thundered the man's voice. Lightning-like flashes burst inside the cavern. Rocked by the force of the words, Juan trembled and his eyes watered, but it wasn't fear he felt. It was a deep welling up of indescribable joy, the recognition of an ancient truth that had always been and always would be. A translucent stream of white shimmered between him and the man.

"We flow in an endless stream," his companion said. "As you stand on the shoulders of those who have come before, you become shoulders for those who follow you. Life is never-ending change. Sachamama sheds one skin at a time and moves forward. What you might see as a mistake becomes an inspiration for your future. Your challenges are opportunities to expand into more of who you are. If you want it and you expect it, creation will bring it to you."

Juan waited for him to finish. He wondered if he was ready to travel to the top of the mountain and find the Snow Star.

"You have journeyed well to reach Apu Ausangate," the man said. "And the Snow Star is where medicine men and women have come since the beginning of time to find their vision. But the domain of the jaguar is where you must travel next. It is where the shaman encounters the mother of all fears, the fear of his own mortality. To pierce the illusion of death is the ultimate act of power for a medicine person. The middle world is about graceful transitions, traveling through life without fear. The jaguar's lagoon is where the shaman rides Otorongo to find this knowledge. When you journey between life and death, you will learn that there is less difference between these states of being than you think."

Juan squirmed. It was hard to imagine riding the beast that killed his llama, even in a vision. The light flickered, and the colors darkened around him. He felt a chill in the room. "There is but one journey from this life into the world of Spirit, Teacher."

"Within this lifetime, there are also many lives," the man said.

"I don't understand," Juan said.

"You began life as a baby, and you grew into the boy who has become a man," he said. "And you will experience other lives, maybe as a husband and a father." The stranger smiled, and Juan saw pink light stream from the man's chest. "A person of power recognizes when it is time for change. A shaman calls upon Otorongo to travel with clarity within a life and between lifetimes."

"And how do I find the jaguar's lagoon?" asked Juan.

"Where the sun returns to earth is where the jaguar laps its dying light. Look for two boulders through which water flows into the basin of a vast lagoon. These powerful *huacas* hold a special portal between the worlds. Leave your claw in Otorongo Q'ocha and depart there before dusk. Otherwise you could rendezvous with more than just your fear of death," said the man. The light in the room grew dim, and his face disappeared into the shadows. The darkness seeped around Juan. But it wasn't the cold that made him shiver. It was the man's warning.

Chapter Twenty-Five

The walls were covered with hoarfrost when he awoke.
A rim of pink trimmed the silhouette of the door. Juan pulled
the blanket around him and crawled over to the fire pit. He
poked through ashes and charred wood to find enough leftover
embers and added twigs until he coaxed out a thin flame. He
threw on a couple of sticks of the split eucalyptus and watched
the fire's delicate blue and yellow fingers wrap around the wood.
He thought about his dream. That man could have been Don
Francisco except he was so much younger than the shaman.

Juan laid a half-dozen potatoes to the side of the coals,
grabbed his tin pot, and headed out the door. The rising sun
edged the peaks of Ausangate with the faint light of dawn and
backlit the overhanging white clouds with a yellow underlay.
Traces of blue ice sparkled through the snow on top of the
peak. He studied the steep rock sides that buttressed the jagged
summit. The main peak dipped down to a lower one on the
eastern side. Don Francisco had told him that the mountain had
been pushed up by deep forces from inside the earth. The front
part lay open with the edge of a glacier field spilling out into a
wall of rock and shale. Soon he would have to climb that wall,
but not today. Today he would follow the path that ran westward.
With a prayer for a safe journey, he lifted his *k'intu* of three coca
leaves to the mountain.

He followed the noisy glacier-fed stream until he found a
natural basin between several large rocks. When he had filled
the pot, he pulled off his cap and stuck his head underneath
the swift current. The water splashed over his neck and down
his chest and back. His scalp tingled with a thousand sharp
pricks. It felt like the bones of his skull parted at their seams.
Screaming, he pulled on his hat, grabbed the pot, and ran back

inside the hut. If his head wasn't clear before, it was now. He sat the pot on the fire and went to check on his fishing line. He could almost smell the trout roasting over hot coals.

The shrub was leaning toward the water when he reached the blue lagoon. Juan untied the line and took out the looseness until he felt a tug at the other end. The fish, circling below, thrashed around before it swam toward the surface. When the silver-skin trout broke through the water and twisted in the air, the rainbow-colored speckles on its sides caught the early morning light. It took a few more leaps before Juan pulled it to shore and landed it with a loud slap against the ground. He gave a silent prayer of thanks to the fish and cleaned it so that the skin held the two halves together in a butterfly-shaped fillet. After he reset the hooks with fresh corn, he threw his line back into Azul Q'ocha. The next fish would be his dinner.

Back inside the hut, he speared the fillet with sharp green sticks and angled it over the coals. He tugged his wool blanket around him and warmed his hands around a cup of coca tea. He watched the embers darken to a deep red and grilled the fish to a light brown. He ate off the sticks, his breath mingling with the vapor of the succulent pink meat. After breakfast, he packed roasted potatoes inside his bag and poured the rest of the tea into his water pouch. It was time to go. From what he could see of the terrain when he hiked up yesterday, he should be back before dark.

Q'inti, a suspended blur of feathers, stared at Juan when he stepped outside. "If it isn't my feathered friend," he said. "It's good to see you again." He took short, quick steps along the path that ran along the glacier stream. When it wasn't darting after an insect, the hummingbird perched on his shoulder and preened itself. When Juan told Q'inti about his dream, it fluttered its wings and squeaked. Stacks of rocks spaced at irregular intervals guided the trail westward.

The sun was at the highest point of the day when they found a pair of boulders worn by the elements into the shape of blunt-edged teeth. They stood like guardians, facing each other across a narrow channel of water that cascaded between them. "These are the *huacas*," he told the bird. "See the marks of the ancient ones."

There was a single hand print carved into each rock. Juan straddled the channel between the two boulders and nestled his fingers into the carvings. His hands trembled with a different vibration from each stone. One was deeper and slower than the other. The left one beat with a drum-like rhythm. The right boulder vibrated with a lighter, higher vibration. Each hand tingled with thousands of tiny pricks. His forehead grew hot before it opened into the passageway of his dream. Shadows, shimmering in the shifting mountain breeze, stepped into the periphery of his vision.

Dressed in bright ceremonial clothing, they crowded around him. Their black hair glistened in the sunlight. They made a warbling sound, similar to the songbirds in the jungle. "We have seen you walking since yesterday," a beautiful young woman said. Thick tresses hung down to her waist.

He hesitated for a moment, surprised that he could understand her words so easily. "Where did you come from?" he asked.

"We live here. This is our home," she said.

"My teacher told me that the ancestors wore long hair like you, but I think that they are much older," he said. The young woman's eyes twinkled, and she covered her mouth. The rest of the group laughed. Embarrassed, Juan started to apologize.

"We enjoy your directness," said the woman. "What else did your teacher tell you about your ancestors?"

"He said that they chose to live in the highest altitudes, in climate where even the hardiest of the Spanish conquistadors dared not venture. He said that their medicine is the most powerful of all."

"Your teacher is wise."

"I am from San Mateo, a village down in the valley. I have come to visit the mountain for a few days," Juan said. "I want to meet my ancestors."

"Perhaps we can help you."

The rest of the group circled around Juan, but he didn't see any of them take a step. Startled by their sudden proximity, he felt a rush of anxiety. Just as quickly, the circle enlarged, again without any apparent movement.

"We did not mean to frighten you," said the woman.

Regaining his composure, Juan nodded. "What can you tell me about these stones?" he asked.

"They are some of the most sacred *huacas* of our people. You have already discovered that each one has a distinct vibration. You can feel it in your fingers. There is a close relationship between the stones and the water. The stones keep the water's vibration harmonious and in balance. Their essence is carried in Puma Rimac that flows through your village and beyond. Your village enjoys the sweetness of the river, no?"

There was something unusual about the way the woman was talking. Her lips were not moving, but her words flowed like the water splashing through the rocks. He could feel what she was thinking.

"Yes you can, just like we feel what you are thinking," she said.

Juan cleared his throat and realized that he also had been talking without using words. But how could he?

"When you touch these stones, you sense our vibrations and we yours," said the woman. "We can feel each other's thoughts more powerfully than any spoken words can convey. When you speak, you create sound, a type of vibration that carries your thought. When you listen, you translate the vibration of my voice into thought. Touch is another way to perceive vibration."

"Each *huaca* has a different vibration," Juan said.

"That's right. These sacred stones share and receive information through their own unique perspective."

Juan took a deep breath. *Why not? Anything was possible.*

"Not only is it possible, but it's easy to understand a *huaca*. You listen and you speak through your touch," she said.

Don Francisco talked with the San Pedro cactus. But it certainly was not through his touch.

"You have many ways that you interpret vibration," said the woman. "Imagine that your touch is like hearing, seeing, tasting, or smelling. Each of your physical senses offers you a different way to experience connection whether you wish to talk to a plant or a stone." She laughed when Q'inti landed on her shoulder and squeaked. "Of course, we must not forget our animal friends."

Juan thought about his animals. He had always just known what they were thinking. It was more of a feeling or a knowing. It was a silent understanding that they shared.

"That's right. Your feelings and your intuition are perhaps the most important ways that you interpret vibration."

But some of the times he saw pictures inside his head, like when he saw through the eyes of the jaguar.

"Yes, the animals often think in pictures. And so do people. You have to be alert because it happens so quickly. It is a wonderful way to talk."

He had heard Don Francisco's voice when he stopped for lunch yesterday even though he was a day's hike away from him. And it could have been the shaman that he spoke to last night in his dream.

"Time and space are not barriers to receiving or sending thoughts. Vibration is the language of the universe. Your thoughts are a powerful way to speak with any aspect of creation."

This woman made everything sound simple. "Who are you?" Juan asked.

"When you feel these *huacas* through the conscious touch of your fingers, you experience who we are," she said. The people of the long hair drew closer. When he looked into their eyes, it was like staring into the sun. The young woman and her friends disappeared into the light. His hands still tingled when he stepped away from the stones. He wished that he could have spent more time with that woman. He had felt such a strong connection with her.

Q'inti circled over the path, and Juan followed the bird along the stream down the mountainside. When they stopped on an outcrop of rock, he saw their destination. The water stretched toward where the earth met the sky. It was Otorongo Q'ocha, the lagoon where the spirit of the jaguar came to drink. A chill rippled through him when he stared into the transparent blue waters below.

Chapter Twenty-Six

The vastness of the lagoon was daunting. The words of the *icaro* sounded braver than Juan felt. "Otorongo, you who lap the light of the dying sun, let me ride upon your shoulders and feel your fur between my legs. Carry me on the journey between life and death that I can travel through life without fear. Show me how to follow the shaman's path with a strong heart and a clear vision."

The jaguar claw that the shaman gave him disappeared with scarcely a ripple into the lagoon. Juan thought about the morning when he first saw the black jaguar. Dark as a moonless night, it had slipped silently through the grass. He had been scared and wanted to run, but he had stayed. He stayed because the yellow eyes told him to. The next time he had looked into the jaguar's eyes, it was over La Reina's broken body. That time they had told him to stand.

The water lapped softly against the shoreline. Afternoon shadows grew longer with the sun's trek into the western sky. The growling in his stomach reminded Juan how much time had passed since breakfast. He finally folded up his *mesa*, grabbed his bag, and sat against a boulder. He broke off a piece of a potato and placed it on the ground with a few drops of water. The hummingbird hopped over, eager to share in his offering to the earth. When he finished eating, Juan stretched out his legs and leaned back against the rock. He thought about what Don Francisco had told him before he left the village.

His sister had been to that cave, and she knew about the storm coming that day. But she went anyway. She must have known that she wasn't coming back. That's why she didn't want him with her. But why did she go? None of it made any sense. It made his head hurt just to think about it. Q'inti fluttered its wings next to his ear. *Just a moment, and then we will go back,* he thought to the squeaking bird. He closed his eyes and crossed his arms across his chest.

A low-throated growl warned him not to move. "What are you looking for?" the beast snarled.

"My name is Juan, and I have made an offering to the lagoon," he stammered.

"I know who you are. I have tasted your essence in my water. Why did you come here, and what do you want?" Its tone suggested that a quick answer would be best.

"My teacher told me that shamans gather their power from this lagoon," he answered.

"And your fear, what is your fear about?"

Juan took a deep breath before he answered. "I am afraid of you, Otorongo," he said. He was surprised by the relief he felt.

"Many say this, but it is not me that you fear. You are afraid of death. I bring its gift only to those who seek it," said the jaguar.

"You are right. I am afraid to die," Juan said.

"It is because you do not understand death. It is much clearer for an animal. It knows that it can travel freely between this world and Spirit. When an animal leaves this life, it knows that it goes to begin another. We do not doubt our eternal nature. Our power lies in the present moment."

"But what about my llama?" asked Juan. "Did she choose to be killed?" He waited for the jaguar's reply. Its silence was worrisome.

"La Reina knew that it was her time to leave," Otorongo finally replied. "She was old, and she had given life to many who carry her proud lineage. It was her choice. It was her time. She was ready. We met as we had agreed."

"But my sister died before she had lived a full life."

"There is no death, only change. Your sister understood this. She never felt the disconnection from Spirit that you have. You came here to understand death. I tell you that it does not exist in the way that you think."

"So what happens when you die?"

"You two-legged ones make it so complicated. You reemerge back into that from which you came, but more than you have ever been," Otorongo growled.

"But where is that?" Juan asked. He regretted the question immediately. An uncomfortable silence followed. The shallowest of breaths moved through his chest. *I must wake up*, he told himself. He took a deep breath and then another until he had cleared his mind of fear. Don Francisco would be proud.

The sun was dropping behind the mountains when he opened his eyes. The boulder was cold against his back. The long shadows of surrounding rocks pointed accusing fingers at him. A chilly wind blew dusty grit across the horizon. Billowy clouds, stained with a blood red color, drifted overhead. It was the hour of power. It was time to return to the hut. With a little luck, he'd have a trout waiting for him at Azul Q'ocha.

He slapped the dust off his poncho and knelt at the edge of the lagoon to wash up. His face cast a dim image in the cold blue water that quivered with the light of the dying sun. He listened, but he heard only the wind. He had no reason to feel spooked. It must be the dream. He splashed his face with the cold water. His scalp rippled and his heart fluttered faster than Q'inti's wings. The moist breath, hot against his neck, stopped him from breathing. Blunt-edged fangs, marked by a lifetime of crunching bones, glistened from the surface of the water. A cold deeper than the depths of the lagoon filled his belly.

The black jaguar stood behind him.

Its yellow eyes studied Juan's reflection. The sunlight narrowed its pupils into dark pinpoints. The vengeful beast must have tracked him up into the mountain. His dream must have been a warning. *It is best to return before the setting sun...* But it was too late. He closed his eyes and pressed his forehead against the ground. He dug his fingers down into the damp soil and wondered how close the jaguar's teeth were to his skull. It had taken but a single grisly crunch to end La Reina's life. That she died quickly was scant consolation.

Gift of the Jaguar

When nothing happened, Juan snuck a peek back at the
lagoon. The jaguar's eyes had dilated in the dimming light. He
tried not to stare into the quivering black centers that floated
inside the yellow rimmed eyes, but they drew him into their
darkness. *Abandon yourself,* he heard. But it wasn't fair. It wasn't
fair that the jaguar decided who died. It wasn't fair that it killed
La Reina. It wasn't fair that Marta knew she would die if she
went to that cave and did it anyway. And it wasn't fair that he had
carried the guilt of her death. And it wasn't fair that the jaguar
was about to kill him now. Juan dug his toes into the ground and
launched himself into Otorongo Q'ocha. His grunt turned into
a scream when he crashed through the water's surface.

Cold clamped his chest like a vise. He swam toward the
nearest side of the lagoon. If he made it before the freezing
water robbed him of his strength, he could find a different way
back to the hut. That jungle cat wouldn't follow him through
the cold water. He heard the angry, staccato roar behind him
and threw his arms forward with heavy strokes and kicked
with a furious desperation. When his legs grew too tired to
move, he paddled but began to sink when his arms gave out.
A mouthful of water made him try harder. With a desperate
kick, his face broke back through the water. He sucked in a
breath of cold air before he sank again. His feeble kick was
not enough to break the surface a second time. When the
darkening water closed over his head, the cold lost its hold on
him. The deeper he sank, the warmer he felt. Bubbles leaked
from his mouth.

The image was a flicker at first, but it grew clearer. There
were people in front of him. It was his family. Rosa was with
them, and she was crying. He wanted to hold her in his arms.

But someone grabbed his poncho from behind and pulled
his head above the water. He spit out a mouthful of water and
gasped. Cold air seared his throat and a fierce burning raged
inside his chest. It had never felt so good or hurt so much to
breathe.

He floated through the water on his back, the poncho tight against the bottom of his chin. He had to get out of the water. It was his only chance. He rolled to his side, wrapped his arms around the thick neck, and pulled himself up onto the jaguar. He looked through the ears swiveling on top of the massive black head and saw that they were heading further out into the lagoon. Its powerful shoulder muscles rippled underneath him as it moved steadily through the water. The jaguar had saved his life. But why and where was it taking him? Exhausted, he dug his fingers into its coat and rested his head on its neck. The warmth of the jaguar's body felt good against his chest. Soon he glided through the water asleep on its back.

The shoreline was green when Juan awoke. He sat up and let his legs dangle over the sides of the jaguar. The water was warm. The jaguar paddled along the shore with its head lifted above the water. Its small ears pointed toward a cove. They floated past trees dense with coca leaves. Hidden in the canopy, faces emerged and then disappeared. Shadowy figures moved in the evening mist. A young woman, holding onto a branch, stretched out her hand. Her finger touched the corner of Juan's mouth, tracing the surprise on his lips.

"I see that you have met Otorongo," the young woman from the rocks said. The jaguar opened its mouth, showing its fangs. She leaned over and scratched him on the snout. "I knew that I could count on you to bring my brother across the lagoon, my old friend, just as you did for me." The cat responded with a combination of a growl and a purr. "Really?" she said. "Is that so?" She laughed.

Juan was confused. He stared at his sister.

"Otorongo said that you were much more trouble than I was," Marta explained.

"I can scarcely believe it's you," he said when he finally found his voice. "I didn't recognize you at first. You are so beautiful. It was you who spoke with me at the *huacas* above the lagoon."

His voice trembled. "You were my big sister, and you said that you would always be there for me," he said. "I prayed to the mountain, but you never came back. You said that the ancestors would bring you home."

"But they did bring me back," she said. "This is where I wanted to be. This is my home, little brother. I couldn't explain this to you before that day of the storm. I knew where I was going, but you wouldn't have understood."

"Don Francisco told me about your dream," he said. "He warned you not to go until you were older."

"He's right," Marta said. "But I couldn't wait. The next time I took the herd to graze, I found the cave on my own. I met one of the ancient ones there. When she told me about Otorongo Q'ocha, I made her promise to bring me here. She said that the jaguar would carry me, but I would have to come alone. I didn't know that it would be the day that you came with me."

His chest ached when he saw how happy his sister was.

"Don't be sad," she said. "I am glad that you came to visit me. And look at you. You are quite a young man now, yes? Happy birthday, Juanito." Marta's laugh was a songbird's warble. "And don't worry. We are never apart. Just put your hand over your heart when you want to feel me. I am always with you."

His sister's face disappeared into the jungle canopy, and the green shoreline faded into dark. "But I want to stay with you," he said. The jaguar's nose pointed toward the open water. It pulled them forward with steady strokes. He laid his head on the cat's neck and let his arms glide through the water. "Perhaps I'm not worthy to stay in the Spirit world," he murmured to the cat. "Maybe I will become part of you now." The beast glided through the water, and Juan fell asleep.

He awoke face down on the damp ground. He pushed himself up onto his elbows and spit the sand out his mouth. The evening wind was quiet, but the cold seeped easily through his wet clothes. He staggered to his feet. He had left the claw that Don Francisco gave him in the lagoon and had awakened with a dream about Otorongo. He'd come back to the water to wash up.

Juan shivered. He wasn't thinking straight. It was too cold. He had to get back to the hut and build a fire. The rest he would think about later. He stumbled backwards when he bent over to pick up his bag. Next to his footprints were deep claw marks around oval depressions in the moist earth. Images of Otorongo and his sister Marta swirled inside his head. He had ridden on the back of the black jaguar to the other side of the lagoon. His sister had touched her finger to his lips and told him things that only she would know. He had to have lost his mind. Marta was dead. But the tracks were fresh, and that jaguar might still be close. He grabbed his bag and ran. With loose rock sliding behind him, he scrambled back up the path toward the stone hut.

Chapter Twenty-Seven

His poncho was stiff with ice. In unmarked stretches, Juan followed the stream when he could not see the path. Uneven steps and protruding rocks caught his toes when he ran. But running was the only time that his teeth stopped chattering. What happened with the jaguar he couldn't think about now. The cold was the greater enemy now. His fingers and toes were numb. He had to find the stone hut. Without a fire, he wouldn't last the night.

When the crescent-shaped moon rose above the mountain, he saw the outline of the thatched roof ahead. He stumbled into the cramped room and stuffed handfuls of dry grass inside the fire pit. His hands shook too much when he tried to strike the piece of flint, and he dropped it. With desperate efforts to feel it in the grass, he found it again. He didn't know if his knuckles or the flint struck the flat piece of metal harder. When a few sparks finally landed on the tinder, he blew until they caught.

With a handful of twigs and a couple of branches, the firelight flickered until it pushed the darkness out from the hut. Juan threw more wood on top of the fire. If he could have stood inside the fire pit, he would have. The glowing mound of orange embers finally forced him back. He pulled off his clothes and wrapped himself in the wool blanket. When he could feel his fingers again, he laid a handful of potatoes near the coals.

The lure of grilled trout beckoned. He could clean the fish by the fire while the potatoes roasted. Wearing a dry pair of pants and a shirt, Juan hurried down the moonlit path. The bush where he had tied his fishing line tilted toward the water's edge. He tugged on the line until he felt the weight at the other end. The line was taut, but the fish hardly budged. To land this one was going to be harder than the last.

Juan dug in his heels, raised the line from the water, and moved one hand over the other. The fish came toward him, but it didn't break the surface. When he leaned back and jerked it out of the water, his feet slipped out from underneath him. He fell on his back, and the fish landed on top of him. It had to be the largest one ever caught from Azul Q'ocha. But it was hard and stiff, and it didn't move.

A bitter taste struggled up from his stomach when he lifted his head. A grinning skull sat on top of a twisted spine with gangly arms and legs sticking out at unnatural angles. Entangled in his fishing line was a human skeleton, and it had his legs pinned against the ground. He kicked it off and leapt to his feet. He flew back up the path to the hut, barreled through the door, and slammed it shut behind him.

He threw more wood on the fire until a thick veil of smoke hung down from the straw thatch. Still the cold clung to him. Huddled underneath the blanket, he tried to sort things out. Something was wrong. Very wrong. He had either lost his mind, or he had just found the remains of a dead man. Or a woman. Shadows danced against the walls. Shifting images of the jaguar, Marta, and the skeleton flickered in front of his eyes.

He had thought all this time that his sister was dead. Or at least she was supposed to be. But Marta lived with the ancestors. He had seen her with his own eyes, and he had talked with her. By the time the branches finally collapsed into dark embers, his eyelids wavered with unbearable fatigue. With more questions than answers, he huddled beneath his blanket and burrowed into the grass. Exhausted, he fell into a deep sleep.

Juan didn't know what part of the night it was when he awakened. He lifted his head. Shadows danced against the stone walls, but there wasn't any fire left in the pit. An elfin-like woman with a short-brimmed white straw hat sat inside his hut. Twin black braids hung in front of a crimson vest embroidered with bright gold thread. She could have been Doña Mariana, except she that was much too young. She was weaving something. One end of the loose strands of yarn was gathered around her waist, and the other end was tied to a long bone braced against the bottom of her feet.

He rolled over onto his elbows for a closer look. Her fingers flew across a brightly lit cloth, tying, shuttling, and weaving it with a deft touch. A stack of bones sat next to her. It was the same way that the women of San Mateo made the ponchos, the blankets, and the clothing for their families. But the yarn that this woman used wasn't hair from alpacas or wool from llamas. It was a very different kind of fiber. These strands of yarn sparkled with an eerie glow. He wanted to tell her that what she was doing couldn't be done.

She was turning light into bones. Bones of all sizes lay around her. Each one was woven with a different pattern. Long ones and short ones, flat ones and round ones, big ones and tiny ones and irregular ones spilled out onto the floor around the weaver. A yellow light poured through holes and flowed across crevices and ridges. He shaded his brow until his eyes could accommodate the brightness. When the woman turned her head, her coppery face shone with a reddish glow. Eyes brimming with light looked up at him. Each one was looking in a different direction.

He went from one to the other before deciding which eye was focused on him. Her lips curved into a shy smile. "You are interested in my work?" she asked. It sounded like the woman was singing when she spoke. Her hands never stopped moving. Juan looked down at the bones lying around the woman and shook his head. Each one vibrated with thousands of tiny sparkles.

"I don't understand," he said. "Where do you get this light from?"

The weaver held a hand over her mouth, but he could see the laughter in her eyes. "Light is energy," she said. "It's everywhere. I collect it from the air. I twist it into cords and spin it around my spindle until I have enough to weave with. Still, it is delicate and it takes a bit of practice to learn to turn it into yarn. The hardest part is adding just enough tension to take the looseness out," she said.

"But how can you make bones out of light?" stammered Juan.

Her lips spread apart, revealing dazzling white teeth. He felt foolish. He had spoken out of turn. "Don't be embarrassed," she said. "You asked a good question. Light is a vibration, an expression of energy that can be woven in a variety of ways. Each bone carries a certain kind of knowledge that depends on how I weave it. Bones have traveled through many ages of creation. And whenever they've needed to change, bones have always risen to the challenge. Wisdom is woven into the very core of their being."

"Bones have wisdom?" Juan asked.

"These bones are *huacas,* keepers of the stories of your people," she said. "They hold the essence of where you come from and the possibilities of who you are becoming. And not just for you but for all creatures. Bones help each animal to move in a way best suited for their particular needs. The hummingbirds, the eagles, and the condors have special bones that allow them the gift of flight. The jaguar has bones that are light but strong enough to support its tremendous muscles. It moves quickly, and it's very agile. But it can't run long distances."

Juan shifted uncomfortably when she mentioned the jaguar, but her smile put him at ease. "People have long legs and short arms," the weaver said. "They can scan the horizon from a high vantage point and walk and run upright for long distances with little need for rest. My work is to make bones that allow the greatest ease of movement for each creature. But, here, let me show you. Watch how easy I make it look," she laughed. With her fingers pulling bands of light from the spindle onto the loom, the woman turned back to her work. Seeing her weave the light into bones still didn't help him to understand how she did it.

"That's the beauty of it," she said. "You don't have to know how it happens. It is the bones' job to understand. You only have to trust their knowing."

"What do you mean?" said Juan.

"It is a special kind of knowledge. It is sensed through feeling. It lies at the deepest level of your being. It is about knowing who you are. Your bones hold your stories and the stories of your ancestors. The energy of Spirit flows through your stories."

"It travels through my bones," Juan murmured. It was what Don Francisco had told him on the morning of his departure from San Mateo.

"Yes," the woman laughed. Her voice vibrated in a high-pitched warble when she spoke. "Just as the stone-lined channels built by ancient ones carried water from the glaciers to the fields far below, your bones channel the energy of Source through you."

"What about the rest of us? What about our eyes, our faces, our skin, our muscles, and our organs?" he asked

The weaver's eyes widened. "These are all wonderful expressions of who you are, inspired by the same intelligence of Source," she said. "In the same way that a family and a village create life around relationships, so you are created. The structure and energy of bone is the innermost part of who you are. Bones are the inner bridges through which movement is created. Each bone connects to its companion through a unique joint, giving you the freedom to move in different ways, in different directions, and for different purposes. The relationship between your bones allows you to be who you are."

Juan watched the currents of light streaming from the room into the woman's hands. Her nimble fingers fluttered like the wings of a hummingbird, gathering strands of light and spinning them around her spindle. She used shuttles of colored crystals to weave the yarn stretched down her legs into bone. She finished a shin bone and fastened it to a thigh bone with ligaments of light.

Swirling, dancing, brilliant streams of light danced past his eyes. The more he tried to follow the light the faster it moved. He sat back on the cut grass and pulled his blanket around him. He heard the whisper of the woman's voice before the blur of her hands spun him back into sleep. "It is enough for now, my young friend, it is enough," she said.

Chapter Twenty-Eight

The morning light streamed in around the edges of the door. When Juan peeked out over the edge of the cover, he saw a wisp of smoke coming from the fire pit. He was torn between getting up and staying underneath the blanket. Finally he rolled out of bed and stepped outside with the blanket clutched around his shoulders. The tip of the sun crested the cloudless mountain summit while he emptied his bladder. A cloud of vapor rose from the ground, and he let out a satisfied breath. He hurried back inside, leaving the door cracked behind him.

He added a couple of sticks of eucalyptus wood and dried dung to the leftover embers. Gnawing on a cold potato, he sipped the leftover tea. It was a strange little woman that sat in his hut last night and wove bones from light. Doña Mariana could have looked like that a hundred years ago. But whose bones were those, and what was their connection with the skeleton that he'd pulled out of Azul Q'ocha? Maybe the weaver had made a new body so that the person could enter into the Spirit world.

"But who died?" Juan asked out loud. He jumped when a flurry of feathers darted underneath his nose. The hummingbird flew up and perched on one of the poles overhead. "Q'inti, where have you been?" he shouted.

Purple feathers puffed out in the center of the tiny green chest. Sparkling violet feathers stuck out like ears from the sides of its head when it looked down at him.

Juan poked a stick into the fire and pushed the ends of the wood deeper into the coals. "I'm sorry that I yelled at you," he mumbled. The bird flew down and landed on his arm. Cocking its head, the bird searched his face. Juan wiped his eyes with his sleeve. "It's the smoke," he said. Q'inti hopped up onto his

169

shoulder and preened its head against the edge of his poncho. The wood had crumbled into dark chunks of reddish gold when he finished talking to the bird, which had squeaked and threatened to fly off whenever his voice rose. He stretched out his arms, and the hummingbird flew to the door. Juan raised an eyebrow. "You want to see if I'm crazy or if there really is a skeleton out there?" he said. The bird fluttered its wings. He shrugged his shoulders and grabbed his bag.

Q'inti hovered in front and squeaked all the way to the lagoon. Squinting in the midmorning sunlight, Juan picked his way through the broken stems of the yellow grass until he stood in front of the bush. It was easy to see his imprint in the muddy ground where he had fallen. He looked at the shrub. His fishing line was still tied to one of the branches. He stared at the lagoon. The hooks at other end of the line lay on the ground near the water. The hummingbird disappeared in a blur of feathers.

"Where is the skeleton?" he shouted, his confusion echoing off the mountain. The thought that it might be him filled his belly with a frighteningly cold sensation. Could he have drowned at Otorongo Q'ocha? How would he know if he was dead? Did ghosts know that they were ghosts? Of course not. That's why they hung around so long, because they didn't know that they had died. They assumed that they were still alive, just like he had. Maybe the jaguar had come and carried his old bones off. The weaver could have woven him a new skeleton out of light so that he could cross over to the world of Spirit. He would stay with Marta after all. But what about Rosa? She said she would wait for him. They were supposed to spend their life together.

Yellow and blue butterflies circled overhead, their colors iridescent in the crisp air. A blue one landed on his nose. Black lines branched out over its wings. "I don't know," Juan said. "I came here to receive a vision for my people, but all I've gotten is more confused." He watched the butterfly lift off with barely a flap or two and circle lazily over his head. White clouds drifted over the mountain's summit, carried by the thermals of the midday sun. Sunlight sparkled off of a patch of blue ice beneath the snowcap. It looked no different than yesterday. Nothing had really changed. That was it. He wasn't dead. He was an idiot. It was all his imagination. His father had warned him about his mind playing tricks on him. It was what drove people to wander the streets of Paucartambo, uttering strange incantations.

Juan sighed and flopped down beside the shrub. He yelped and jumped to his feet when he felt the sharp prick. The pointed tip of a claw stuck up from the ground. He wiped it off and held it up to the light. It had a hole in the bottom where it had hung around his teacher's neck. It was the claw that Don Francisco had given him. He swore that he had thrown it into Otorongo Q'ocha. Maybe the jaguar had left it and carried off the skeleton.

Q'inti's sudden appearance startled him. The purple-masked bird hung like an ornament in front of his face. Tiny golden sparkles danced on the edges of its wings. Droplets of sunlight trickled off the feathers. The trickle became a ripple that became a wave. Waves of light crested, one after another. Each passing swell lifted Juan higher than the previous one. He couldn't breathe fast enough. "It's too much," he said. "I can't."

Relax, Juanito. Relax and enjoy the ride, he heard.

"Marta, is that you?" he asked.

"Allow the energy to move through you, little brother. It will carry you. Don't try so hard. Follow the flow and it gets easier," she said. A stream of bubbles moved through his muscles. His eyelids blinked, and his arms and feet began to twitch. His body had a mind of its own. The earth spun underneath him. No, he was the one who was moving. He was spinning into formlessness, dissolving back into pure light. He was moving through space without a body.

He must have died at Otorongo Q'ocha. Only now was he able to experience the journey to the afterlife. His sister was taking him home with her. The wind whispered past him. Riding on currents of warm air, he felt light and clear. He opened his eyes, and he saw Ausangate. But he was near the crest of the mountain, and the lagoon was a sparkling blue patch below.

"I am soaring over Azul Q'ocha," he shouted. A loud *cree* echoed off the mountain. The fluttering tips of an eagle's wing feathers stretched out on both sides of him. *"Cree, cree,"* he cried again. Juan spiraled up the rising afternoon thermals in lazy circles. When he wanted to turn, all he had to do was point his eyes where he wanted to go. His wings and the wind did the rest. The next time he flew past the mountain's peak, he looked down. He was dead. There was nothing that he couldn't do. He tucked his wings next to him and rolled into a steep dive, plummeting to the earth in a nearly vertical line. Just before he reached the ground, he extended his wings and his tail feathers. He flapped his wings and rode the warm air currents back to the top of the mountain.

"Feel the air pushing underneath your wings. Hardly a feather moves, Juanito. You are an eagle that knows its own instinctive balance of structure and energy. When you fly wingtip to wingtip with Spirit, this is what it feels like." He rode the thermal currents until even Ausangate disappeared beneath him. Effortlessness flowed through the core of his being. No longer conscious of flying, he heard only the distant sound of a beating heart.

"You can fly as high as you want when you are grounded in who you are," his sister said. "You are traveling on the leading edge of creation. Spirit finds its greatest joy through your experiences and through those of all sentient beings. Honor your own life. It is your gift, my brother. Share from who you are when you seek to teach others."

"But where am I?" Juan asked.

"You have traveled to the north side of the mountain. One enters this domain when embraced by a passion to uplift others. A shaman becomes a guide for those who want to find their own connection to Spirit. He rekindles their passion to dream and to create their own destiny. The wise healer understands that reality begins in the imagination. The most precious legacy that you give another is to inspire them to follow their dreams. A strong desire can move a mountain if a person believes it is possible.

The story they tell will create the path they travel. This is destiny and each person creates their own."

The high-pitched humming faded, and Juan circled downward. He spun in a tighter and tighter circle before he flared and landed on the ground with a light touch. Q'inti circled around his head, paused in midair, and touched his nose with its beak. The hummingbird squeaked before it left to chase insects that skittered across shadows lengthening on the surface of the lagoon.

Chapter Twenty-Nine

He remembered how his sister and he had pretended to be different animals when they were kids. It was another one of her games. She called it shape-shifting. Their mother had taught his sister how, but Marta wasn't supposed to tell Juan. It was a secret. He would have to wait until he was older before she could really show him how to do it. But it was okay if it was only play-like, she had said.

When he and Rosa had stretched out their arms underneath the soaring eagles, he never imagined that it could ever be anything other than a children's game. But she must have known shape-shifting was possible. Her grandfather must have shown her this when she was growing up.

Rosa came to her grandfather's house when he stayed there before his trip. She and Don Francisco had talked too low to hear much, but Juan had caught a glimpse of her lips. She had said something about him learning how to "travel in dreamtime". They had no doubt planned for years for him to come to the sacred mountain. Don Francisco must have known that Ausangate was the only way to show him what he had already taught his granddaughter.

Juan shaded his eyes and squinted to see the strange-looking bird that glided along the side of the lagoon still lit by the afternoon sun. It was a horned coot that shoveled its bill along the rocks. The black creature, with a forward-pointing, muscular fleshy organ on its forehead, was building a small island out of stones in the shallow edges of the water. His father had told him that it did this to keep its nest safe from predators. It tugged at one particular rock along the shore without much success. Finally it gave up and paddled back to its nest.

He walked along the shore to where the coot had been at
work. He leaned over and pulled out a fist-sized gray circular
stone. It had a hole in the middle, similar to one in Don
Francisco's house. It was a medicine stone used by the ancient
ones to grind certain plants to make teas for vision, the shaman
had told him. Even when the center wore through, the spirit of
the plant medicine was left in the stone. It was a window into
other worlds, those beyond physical time and space, he had said.

Juan tried to imagine that the stone was a portal through
time. He thought about the soaring condors woven into the
blue tapestry on Don Francisco's wall when he blew onto the
stone. He held the rock against his forehead. It softened until it
felt like it had molded itself against his skull. A stiff breeze blew
across the lagoon, and light-dappled ripples slipped through
the dark blue water. *Time is unmoving yet moved through,* he heard.
Triangles, circles, curves, and other geometric symbols flashed by
him, vibrating light.

The smell of the jungle-grown *mapacho* hung in the air. Juan
softened his eyes, and the space around his teacher opened.
Don Francisco tamped his thumb down into the green bowl
of his long-stemmed pipe and lit the tobacco with a burning
ember. A rainbow of colors shifted around him when he moved
or gestured. It was just like the man in his dream. The shaman
smiled. "Your vision has grown strong on the mountain," he
said. "You are ready to work with the light body that surrounds
a person. Or you can work directly with the physical body. Both
ways are good," he said.

"Teacher, is it possible to work with both at the same time?"
Juan asked.

Don Francisco blew the smoke underneath his hat and over
himself before he blew it into the lower, middle, and upper
worlds. "When you were a little boy, you rescued a baby gopher,"
he said. "You took it home, and you breathed into its mouth and
tried to give it back its life. And then there was the day of the
summer solstice ten seasons ago. You picked a basket of fresh
corn from your mother's garden, and you fed it to the alpacas,
llamas, cows, and donkeys of your family's herd. You sang at the

top of your voice when you gave each of them an ear of corn. I saw you." He chuckled. "Not that your mother was too pleased when she found out. But then again, Wilhelmita encouraged your love of animals."

The shaman's opaque eyes grew misty. Juan saw memories of a distant past settle upon him like clouds that hung over the mountain's crest. He watched him drift into another time. After a long silence, Don Francisco shook his head. "When you take the livestock up into the high pastures, the horses and cows travel up the steep, narrow trail single file, bumping into each other when they're pushed," he said. "And the alpacas and llamas jostle behind each another in much the same way. But the burros, they..."

"Lean into each other," said Juan.

"They lean into each other, and it allows them to climb with less effort," he said. "Even the simple burro likes to feel supported. To give their weight to each other on a narrow cliff is trust at its deepest, most instinctual level. If you touch people in this way, they can stop their struggle for a moment and relax into their natural state of well-being. And their path becomes easier. I call it donkey touch. You help them to feel the essence of that which they are, the energy of Source flowing through flesh and bone."

"Where would I start?" asked Juan.

"I believe that bone is a good place to work with the physical body and the energy body at the same time," said Don Francisco. "We are built around our bones. If you support people with donkey touch at the center of their being, you could help them find their way back home. When they find harmony with that which they are, they will heal themselves."

"Can you teach me how to work in this way?"

"You've shed the skin of a painful past at the cave, and the serpent spirit cleansed your energy body at the hot springs," the shaman said. "You released your physical body at Otorongo Q'ocha with the help of the jaguar spirit. And you've tasted the sweet nectar of the wisdom of our ancestors through the hummingbird and your sister Marta. Indeed, you have learned much that will serve you well as a healer and a teacher. Perhaps this would be enough for most. But to access the highest realms of understanding, you must travel to the upper world, to the place of the Snow Star. To see through the eyes of the condor can only come from direct experience in the *hanakpacha*."

Don Francisco pursed his lips and exhaled. "Prepare your *despacho* and ask for Spirit to show you the way. It will not be easy, and not all who go are able to find it. Start early in the morning. There is a shallow bowl that lies beneath the summit. You will see a pool nestled between the rocks. Be there before the sun rises above the peak. Listen to your heart and hear the voice of the mountain. Call upon Hatun Kuntur and ask to see beyond the world of space and time. From the back of the condor, you can glimpse into eternity and see life from a higher perspective."

"And then?" Juan asked.

"Then you will have your answer," said the shaman. "And if we are fortunate, you will return to San Mateo by nightfall tomorrow."

The blue tapestry with soaring condors that hung on the shaman's wall faded into the lagoon. The old man's words echoed in the wind that swept across Azul Q'ocha. When the round stone with the open portal dropped back into Juan's hand, he stared up at Ausangate. It was time to travel to the top of the mountain.

Chapter Thirty

Juan studied the snow-capped peaks and wondered how long a man could last up there. His sister had taught him to pray to the sacred mountain. Their people had always prayed to the *apus*. Each breath and every step that he took on the way to the top would be a prayer.

A trout leapt from the water, slapping it with its tail. Juan baited his hooks with corn and swung the fishing line over his head. When he let it go, the weighted end plopped into the water close to the fish. With hands clasped behind his back, he walked along the shoreline and thought about what Don Francisco had said. It would take a keen touch to feel energy that flowed like water through hard bone. Maybe it would feel like the vibration in the sacred stones that stood above Otorongo Q'ocha, where he first met the ancestors.

The hummingbird buzzed his head before it landed on his shoulder. "What do you think, Q'inti?" he asked. The bird cocked its head to one side. "I know," he said. "It is an interesting thought, but can I grow potatoes with it? That's the question my father would ask." He tugged absentmindedly on the cords of his peaked hat until he had it pulled down over his brow. The furrow between his eyebrows deepened. "Of course," he said. "That's it." The hummingbird darted off and perched on the branch where the fishing line was tied. The tip of the branch touched the water.

Hesitant, Juan held the line with both hands and added just enough tension until he felt movement at the other end. Satisfied that he had a fish, he pulled it in with an easy give-and-take motion until a good-sized rainbow trout flopped onto the shore. "It's like the tension in the fishing line," he explained to the bird. "When I first took the line in my hands, I knew that I

179

had hooked something heavy at the other end. I was hoping that it was a fish, but I couldn't be sure until I took up enough slack to feel it move at the other end. When I engaged the line with more tension, my delicious friend and I enjoyed a meaningful conversation about whether he would join me for dinner. Of course, if I pulled too hard or too soon, the trout might have leapt off my hook."

The hummingbird lighted on his shoulder. Juan removed the backbone and ribs from the trout, leaving a butterfly-shaped pink fillet. "Don Francisco said I could work with a person's light body through their bones. Do it with a 'donkey touch' they can lean into, he said. Maybe what works with a donkey and a fish could work with a person." Q'inti tilted its head. Its squeak sounded like a question.

"It's like a handshake," Juan said. "Too weak and it makes the person uneasy. Too strong and they pull away. With just the right amount of pressure, a handshake can create trust without a word being spoken. If I could just find a way to do this through a person's bones..." He imagined sharing his thoughts with Don Francisco and Rosa. They would laugh, but at least they wouldn't think he was crazy. Or maybe they'd be glad that he was.

He broke off a stem of *muña* and rubbed it across his lips. He remembered the day that he and Rosa climbed the hill to bury their stone. They were only five years old, but she was right. He had promised her that one day, when they were grown-ups, they would return to dig it back up. Rosa and he would have much to talk about when he returned to San Mateo.

Twilight had cast its dim light over the mountain by the time he returned to the hut. Gusting winds, in their hour of power, rattled the straw thatch. Juan staked the filleted trout near a bed of coals, set the rest of his potatoes beside it, and added a handful of coca leaves to the boiling water. It was time to make his *despacho*. He spread a plain white paper against the earthen floor and laid out enough coca leaves to make *k'intus*.

He prayed over Doña Mariana's neatly bundled packets of dried kernels of corn, anis, quinoa and other seeds, llama fat, a thumb-sized llama, an assortment of sweets, and tiny replicas of

gold and silver coins. He made a circle from the *k'intus*, praying
for Rosa, Don Francisco, his family, Doña Mariana, the people of
San Mateo, and himself. He opened each packet and layered the
ingredients inside the circle, offering each item to Pachamama
and to the mountains. From a small vial, he sprinkled brandy-
like *pisco* over the gifts. He folded the paper into a tight bundle
and tied it with string. He stacked the rest of the wood into
the fire pit and laid his *despacho* on top. Flames licked around
his offering, and smoke carried his intentions for a successful
journey into the upper world.

Outside the hut, he aligned his *q'uyas* on the blue *mesa* cloth
that Rosa had made him. The yellow triangular stone from the
serpent spirit sat to the south. Juan laid the claw from Otorongo
on the west side. In the north, he placed the round medicine
stone from Azul Q'ocha. He put his father's condor on the east
side of the *mesa*. In the center of the cloth he set Don Francisco's
pouch. Embroidered with rows of finely stitched stars, it held the
stone that his teacher had received from the Snow Star. Around
it he placed the *q'uyas* given him by the elders on the morning he
began his journey to the mountain.

The first star twinkled in the evening sky when he stood over
his *mesa* and lifted up his hands to Ausangate. He summoned the
guardian spirits from the lower, middle, and upper worlds. He
sang to Q'inti. It was the hummingbird that came to him and his
mother that morning in the garden when she had shared about
Don Francisco's reading of the leaves. It had kept him headed in
the right direction on his journey to the mountain. It embodied
his sister's spirit, carrying her words from another world. And it
was a friend that listened when there was no one else to
hear him.

With wings vibrating in the dying light, the hummingbird
cast a finely etched silhouette over his *mesa*. A green feather
tipped with purple drifted down and landed on top. The bird
peered into his eyes, its beak barely touching his nose. This part
of the journey was his alone to travel. Q'inti would not be going
with him tomorrow. When the hummingbird disappeared into

the night air, Juan knew that he would have to listen to his own guidance now. His life depended on it.

The wind had died to a bare whisper when he tucked in the corners of the *mesa* cloth and went back inside. He washed down the last bite of fish with tea and packed up the leftover potatoes for the trip home. Wrapped inside his blanket, Juan fell into a restless sleep. Lost in fields of snow and ice, he turned from one side to the other, searching for the elusive Snow Star.

Chapter Thirty-One

The crescent moon hung over the western horizon when he stepped outside the hut. The four stars of the Southern Cross and the Eyes of the Jaguar were still visible. He shivered in the cold air, but he took the time to find the other constellations. The crest of Ausangate towered above him, its white peaks a dim temple against the dark sky. He finished his potato in a couple of bites. There wasn't enough time to build a fire. Two *q'uyas* were all that he would carry with him. The rest of his gear he would pick up when he got back.

Juan rubbed his face and blew into his hands. The moisture from his breath dissipated into the dry air. There was no path to the summit. There was only a steep mound of slick gray rock and loose gravel, shed from the mountain like a protective wall. It had to be the height of ten men. He wedged his fingers and dug the toes of his sandals into the rock. It was hard work in the loose footing. He would slide part-way down and scramble back up to gain another few yards. The dust coated his mouth and left his throat raw. By the time he reached solid footing, the tips of his toes and fingers were numb, and his muscles had begun to cramp. His heart thudded against his ribs. His chest would burst if he took another step.

With his hands braced against his knees, he stared at the lagoon nestled into the side of the mountain. He thought it would be more. It was scarcely a pond. A white boulder stood above it on the uphill side. Minerals, leached into the water, colored it with a milky white patina. A crystalline layer of ice floated on top. A rock on the near side of the lagoon would make a good seat.

Even sitting, it was hard to pull in enough air. His lungs ached for more oxygen. But he could do no more than fill and empty his chest in the dark quiet of the mountain and wait. And shiver. The wind was quiet this morning, but still his face burned from the cold. He rocked back and forth, stamped his feet and kept his hands jammed into his armpits underneath his poncho. He was colder than he had ever been.

Morning tiptoed over the crest of the mountain with an aura of faint light.

The white peaks of the Cordillera Vilcanota range stretched out like giant wings on both sides. Juan took in each crevice, nook, and cranny on the craggy face of Ausangate. Below the tallest peak, beneath the ice and snow, was a heart-shaped outcrop. The sun rose over the glacier cap, and streaks of red clouded his vision. Unable to bear the blinding light, Juan shielded his eyes and looked down toward the pool. Tinkling with the sound of a tiny bell, cracks spread through the thin layer of ice. The rays of the sun, filtered through the mineralized water, split apart. The crystalline lagoon vibrated with shades of turquoise, blue, indigo, and violet.

Marta had told him the legend, but now he saw it for himself. It was Alca Q'ocha, the Rainbow Lagoon. The sun climbed above the peak, transforming the rock on the other side of the water into a glistening white crystal. It had to be the Snow Star. Juan rubbed his face, his hands, and his feet with his poncho until he felt his skin sting from the coarse weave. He hobbled toward the boulder-sized crystal on sore feet. He opened the pouch that the shaman had given him. Polished into the shape of a heart, the crystal rolled into his hand. The mountain itself had given Don Francisco this *q'uya*. It was the centerpiece of the shaman's *mesa*. Juan laid it on a shallow ledge carved into the altar. Next to the pink crystal he sat the black stone carved into a condor that his father had given him.

The three coca leaves that he offered were dry and fragile. They were all that he had. One was for the lower world and one was for the middle one. And the last was for the upper world where the condor soared wingtip to wingtip with Spirit. He rested his hands and his head against the crystal altar and prayed to the mountain. The words of his *icaro* came out in a sing-song warble.

"I met Sachamama in the hot springs of Pacchanta," he said. "In Otorongo Q'ocha, I rode the back of the jaguar. Now I ask to fly with Hatun Kuntur. On the back of the condor, let me peek into eternity to see the destiny that waits for me." He sang to All That Is and gave thanks to the plant people, the stone people, the two-legged, the four-legged, the many-legged, those that burrow, swim, fly, crawl, and run. He sang to Rosa, asking that their wingtips would always touch. He sang for his family, Don Francisco, Doña Mariana, and all the people of San Mateo. His thanks to Mother Earth, Grandmother Moon, Father Sun, and the Star People said that he too was part of the light of creation. And he prayed for the children: the born, the ready-to-be born, the still-born, and the never-born.

He could hardly breathe. But his heart could burst for all he cared. He knew that Marta would always be with him. She had told him so. Even with the cold, he had never felt more alive. He could sing forever and die a happy person. *The ecstasy that you feel is the appreciation that creation has for you*, he heard. That the voice came from inside of him made the words feel that much better.

He felt the altar humming against his hands and his forehead. His fingers and nose tingled and grew warm. The crystal became too hot to touch, and he was forced to step back. Light from the altar flowed through the pink crystal. The focused beam shone on the heart-shaped outcrop below the peak. A cleft opened in the middle of it. He had to climb up a nearly vertical rock face to get there.

Juan pulled himself up the mountain, wedging his fingers into cracks, and finding footholds where he could stand. He moved a hand and then a foot at a time. The cold seared the bleeding tips of his fingers and toes. When his hacking cough threatened his hold on the mountain, he rested on a narrow rock ledge halfway up to catch his breath. But he couldn't stay too long. His muscles were cramping, and he could barely grip anything with his fingers. His body was heavy and stiff, but still it moved. It felt like the mountain was pulling him up its face to the mouth of the cave.

When he crawled through the opening, his vision, still blurred from the sun, was slow to adjust in the dark. Dagger-like icicles, shimmering with a dim light, hung from the ceiling. When the low growl echoed inside the cave, Juan knew that he wasn't alone. The jaguar stepped out from the darkness. It was Otorongo, its black coat almost blue. Its yellow eyes bored into his. Death had come to meet him once again.

Juan looked into the jaguar's eyes. *Abandon yourself,* he heard. The yellow orbs of the beast flickered until the two eyes became one. Its black coat glowed until the jaguar was pure light. When the one became two eyes again, they were blue. And the vibrating light coalesced into a human form. The jaguar had become his teacher. Don Francisco, encircled in a pale halo, hovered above the cave floor.

The deep rolling thunder that shook the mountain knocked Juan onto his back. Stones cracked against stones. Rocks cascaded down the mountain until the sound was a roaring crescendo. He felt a strong curve move through his bones. He was weightless. From the top of his head to the bottom of his feet, a wave of energy flowed like spring run-off from the mountains. The shaman's voice echoed inside the cave.

"Energy moves in curves," he said. "When you engage others from their feet with a pull curved like the crescent moon, you touch not only their bones, but you help them to remember who they are. When you connect them with their energy body, you remind them that they are Spirit flowing through a physical body. This is where the deepest healing takes place.

"Spirit expands with your dreams. Each person comes into this world to live that which their dreams call them to become. Use the curve of the crescent moon to bring others into harmony with their dreams, to the place where Spirit dwells.

"Spirit travels through you in each breath and in each heartbeat. And when it passes through you, it is imprinted with who you think you are. You are constantly being made and remade in each moment according to your thoughts. What you think, you attract into your experience. This is *ayni.*

"The first job for all people is to be who they are. Then they can seek their destiny from a place of knowing. Tell this to those who come to you for healing. Tell them that they are the gift that they are searching for."

The rumbling still echoed when Juan opened his eyes. The tomb-like cave was empty except for pieces of ice and rock scattered across the floor. He knew that he had to get out. The aftershocks could bring down enough rock to bury him. He crawled out on his stomach, lowered himself over the ledge, and jammed the edge of his sandal into a shallow groove. He almost had a second toehold in the slick rock when one of his hands slipped off. Stretched across the face of the mountain, he couldn't reach up, and he couldn't step down. His hand slid toward the edge.

His father was right. This mountain wanted all of you, body, mind, and soul. There would be no going back to San Mateo. His life had condensed into this single moment. He had no choice. There was nothing he could do about it. He couldn't hold on any longer. His last finger slipped from the slick rock.

The wind slapped the loose end of his poncho against his face. Juan couldn't hear his own voice when he fell. He clawed and kicked at the air in a desperate attempt to right himself. He couldn't see whether he faced up or down. His free fall ended with a jarring impact against his back. The first bounce knocked the breath out of him. After the second and the third ones, everything went dark. He felt nothing, and he heard nothing. He was afraid to move. The broken bones would be unbearable when the shock wore off. But the cold would be a merciful friend and take the pain away when his body became numb. He slid the poncho from his face. At least one arm still worked. He opened one eye and then the other.

He dug his hands into the downy white feathers around the base of the bald head and pulled himself up, tucking his legs inside the black plumage on the bird's back. With its long wings stretched out and its dark red comb pointed up, the Andean condor soared over the mountain's peak. Its white-tipped wing feathers shimmied when it climbed through the early morning skies but steadied when they had reached the deepest blue of the earth's atmosphere. Juan pulled himself deeper into the feathers.

Feel my heart, he heard. *Remember this moment.* Rosa's laughter rang in his ear. He felt her hands grab onto his waist. Her breath warmed the back of his neck. Together they rode the condor through space, curving around the earth along a path of light. They soared over vast stretches of water and lands filled with peoples of different colors. A web connected each person to the path that circled the earth. Whenever their color brightened, the circle pulsed and expanded its rainbow arc of light. The condor's wingtips nearly brushed the snow-capped peaks on the other side of the world. The mountains reminded him of the Andes. The people there even looked like those of San Mateo, but they wore unusually long wool robes. Their cows were bigger and had shaggy coats and horns that curved up and back.

Hatun Kuntur climbed up into the blackness beyond earth. Juan no longer felt Rosa pressed against his back. Whether he shivered from the cold or from ecstasy, he didn't care. Such an intense joy filled his chest that it ached. All was light and he was light. *You are not separate from that which we are. Your light is part of creation.* The black spaces between the bodies of light expanded into more light with each burst of appreciation he felt. It was joy that created this ever-expanding universe. And it was his destiny to serve in the way of his ancestors, to help others to discover their light.

When he opened his eyes, his face was pressed against the altar. The heart-shaped crystal sat next to his hand. It had changed color from pink to a deep green. Juan held it to his chest. He felt its vibration and heard the voice of his teacher.

"Your heart is now one with the mountain and with mine. Take this crystal and remember that all well-being comes from Spirit and that all things are possible. Meet others where they stand in the present moment, without judgment. See them with your heart, knowing where each of you ends and the other begins. Trust their natural well-being to emerge when they feel your support. Show them how to find the sacred space within themselves. When they sense their Inner Being, they will reconnect to who they are. And when they feel this, they will discover that the gift that awaits them is who they have become."

The Rainbow Lagoon was a milky white color, and the altar was a stone again. Juan tucked the green crystal and the carved condor into his bag and eased himself up. He stood for a moment, looking for the cave, but it had disappeared into the rock face. When he turned around, he saw that the Puma Rimac cut a thin blue path through the yellow grasslands below. Inkawari, dotted with green and yellow squares, was a distant rise at the other end of the vast *altiplano*. He imagined that the white wisp on the horizon was smoke from the cooking fires of the village. He would tell Rosa how small San Mateo looked from the top of Ausangate but that it was no less precious. Juan felt the warmth of the sun on his back when he started down the side of the mountain.

Chapter Thirty-Two

Clouds started to close over the summit at the moment that he sat on his poncho and slid down the loose rock. It took little time to reach the stone hut. Juan stayed only long enough to coat his toes and fingers with his mother's salve and to gather the rest of his gear. It was important to stay ahead of the high-altitude weather. He had been fortunate the last few days, but he knew that the conditions on the mountain could rapidly change. He wouldn't stop to rest until he reached lower elevations. His unrelenting dry cough and queasy stomach would do better farther down. He made his way across the tundra to the trail below.

The moving shadow shortened and lengthened across the uneven terrain and passed over his head. The bird spiraled downward, tilting its ponderous wings from side to side before it landed on top of a boulder. Huge talons gripped the granite like bony fingers. Juan picked his way through the loose rock, grimacing each time one of his big toes bumped up against a stone. The condor stretched out its wings when he neared its perch, brushing his face with its feathers. Its wingspan was longer than he was tall. The ruff of white feathers that surrounded the base of the nearly featherless neck were yellowed and frayed. The dull red color of its head and wattle brightened when it looked down at him. It stretched out its neck, and with the tip of its craggy beak the bird touched the top of his head.

It was an understanding beyond words. There was nothing more important than being who he was becoming. Everything was of Source and was Source. There was no separation. He was an eternal being constantly growing in the endless spiral of the *pachacuti*. His life was part of Spirit's dance through time. His songs carried the tune. His love, freed from longing and regret,

191

made the music sweeter. *Feel it in your bones, because you cannot hold it all in your mind,* he heard. He lifted his face and saw his worthiness reflected back a thousand times in the condor's eyes. *You are your own teacher,* they said.

The condor stretched out its wings, and the long black feathers brushed over him with a heavy rush of air. Lifted by the groundswell, it began to pull away from the rock. When its wings caught the rising thermals, the bird circled up until it soared above the peaks of Ausangate. Juan watched the v-shaped wings fade into an invisible dot over the eastern horizon.

Two black wing feathers lay against his feet. One was for him, and the other was for Rosa. She had always believed that the ancient healing ways would live through them. It was she who had beckoned him to explore the hills around the village when they were kids. It was she who had kept the dream alive after Marta's death. She was the one who had insisted that he talk to her grandfather and encouraged him to follow the shaman's path. And she had given him the greatest gift that anyone could offer another. She believed in him.

Don Francisco was right. The trip had taken three days, but his journey would last a lifetime. Ausangate had become his home, and many seeds had been sown during his stay. But it would take time to grow corn from all that he had experienced. He still had much to learn from Don Francisco before he was ready to be a healer for the people of San Mateo.

He followed the trail down the mountain and imagined the barrel-chested shaman in the black poncho and the brown felt hat with an eagle feather that dangled behind. Don Francisco would be standing on the banks of Puma Rimac where they had last spoken. With sinewy arms that were more bone than flesh, his talon-like fingers would lift his staff above his head. The fierce pride in those eagle-sharp eyes would say well done in a way that few words could.

The sun shone directly overhead when he reached Pacchanta. He thanked the serpent spirit, but he made it clear that a bath was all he needed. When his skin started to wrinkle, he slipped out of the water back into his clothes. He ate his last potato and stretched out to soak in the heat of the afternoon sun. With his eyes closed, he saw Rosa reach out to him with tears in her eyes. Villagers paraded through the streets, playing music. His parents hugged him and his brother and sisters shouted.

It was mid-afternoon when he awakened. With a mostly empty blanket on his back, he scrambled down the white rocks to the trail below. The light had deepened to a golden yellow around Inkawari Mountain when he reached the grass-covered plateau. The herds had already returned to the village. Late afternoon gusts of wind fell to an easy breeze.

Evening clouds picked up a reddish trim as Juan kept his pace through the tough yellow clumps of *ichu*. They changed to shades of purple before he picked out the Southern Cross and the Eyes of the Jaguar in the night sky. He was anxious to get home, but his sore feet kept him from walking any faster. The smell of roasted corn and wood smoke wafted up from the village when he started down the switchbacks to the Puma Rimac. The din of drums, flutes, and bells grew louder the closer he got. The people of San Mateo were calling him back to the village. It was what he had seen in his vision.

He tucked his hair underneath his hat, slapped the dust off his poncho, and picked up his feet. When he reached the river, a dim silhouette stood on the far side and waved to him. It was Rosa who stepped out from the shadows. He picked his way across the rocks and jumped up onto the bank. Her face caught the moonlight. She was crying. "He lives through us now," she whispered. "He loved us so much."

Water splashed against stone, and music drifted on the night breeze. Juan took Rosa into his arms. "Don Francisco had already seen his own death when he warned me about the coming changes for our village," he said.

"My grandfather waited until he knew you had found the Snow Star," she said. They stood in silence, heart beating against heart.

Villagers paraded through the streets, banging drums, shaking rattles, and playing flutes. Juan looked at Rosa, confused. Doña Mariana shuffled up to him. The blue-tinged eyes, looking in different places, greeted him warmly. "The loud music is to remind him not to return to his body," she said. "It was his time to go. He would want to know that you are happy for him."

He and Rosa walked to his house, stopping to receive hugs, handshakes, and kisses. When they reached his family's home, Maria and Anna ran out to greet them. They grabbed his arms and shouted, each one trying to get his attention. His brother stepped out from the house and slapped him on the back. Wilhelmita wiped her hands on her apron before she locked her heavy arms around him. His father shook his head when his mother rocked Juan back and forth with warbled sounds of mothering.

"Give the poor boy some room to breathe," Humberto protested.

Juan caught his father's eye. "Thanks for what you did," he said.

Humberto nodded. "We missed you," he said.

José grabbed Juan from behind and they scuffled, each trying to take off the other's hat. His mother took his brother by the arm and made everyone come inside.

His sisters chattered nonstop. "Did you miss us? Were you scared? What did you see? What did you do?" Their questions came out one on top of the other.

"Hush," Wilhelmita told them. "Your brother's tired. You can ask him about his trip tomorrow." She handed him a bowl of quinoa soup with a white potato in the middle.

"It's okay," Juan said. "I've missed hearing these two songbirds." When he tugged on Anna's braids, Maria held up one of hers for him to pull. José made faces at them, laughing when they shook their fingers at him.

"You still make the best soup in all of San Mateo," Juan mouthed to his mother. She wrapped her arms around his neck and buried his face against her chest. Wood smoke and garlic had never smelled better. From the corner of his eye, he saw Humberto smile.

"Papá, have you thought any more about how we should plant our fields next season?" he said.

His father's face brightened. "I was thinking that we could plant barley in the upper fields. We'll plant the potatoes lower down. It will make less work for us come harvest time," he said.

The rest of the family was sleeping soundly when Juan returned from Rosa's. Blankets were spread over a straw mat on the other side of the room. "Good night," he whispered. Nestled underneath layers of alpaca wool, the dreams began before he could close his eyes.

Chapter Thirty-Three

Light radiated through the dark blue skies. Juan ran behind the alpacas and llamas. Marta stood on top of a polished white rock. She looked almost transparent. "Juanito, come here," his sister called out. The puma's roar shattered the peacefulness of the early morning and scattered the herd. He ran toward his sister. She laughed when he leapt up onto the rock and lay by her side. With a purr-like growl, he arched his back against his sister's hand. "It is good to see you happy again," she said and stroked his tawny coat. Only a distant voice disturbed his deep contentment.

"Wake up. You're having another dream, Juanito," his mother whispered. She shook his shoulder a second time. Juan stretched out his arms and yawned. "I was with Marta," he said. He looked at his mother and smiled. "Let me have a cup of tea, and I'll explain." Wilhelmita's concern turned into a look of confusion.

It was late by village standards when his mother tipped the dented copper kettle and poured hot water over the coca leaves. His father had already gone to the fields, and José had taken the herd up to the high pastures to graze for the day. His sisters played outside, arguing over which one would lead the way to the sacred mountain this morning. Wilhelmita handed him a cup of steaming tea, and Juan took careful sips between bites of corncakes dipped in honey. He licked his fingers and watched Wilhelmita add dried potatoes to a pot of boiling water. He waited until she faced him.

His mother studied his face. Her eyes clouded over with an anguish that he understood all too well. "It's about Marta," she said.

Juan nodded. "I saw her," he said. "She lives with the ancestors and watches over us in ways that we can scarcely imagine." His mother pulled him against her chest, spilling his tea. He laughed and held the cup away from him. "Careful or you will burn us both," he said. With her attention on his lips, he took his mother on his journey to Ausangate. There was a faraway look in her eyes when he was done. "Tell me what happened with Don Francisco," he said.

Wilhelmita dabbed at her eyes with her apron. "There is a meeting of the village elders tonight," she said. "Humberto said that they want to talk with you and Rosa. There's been much discussion about Francisco José's passing and what it will mean for the people now that he is gone." Juan didn't say anything. He softened his eyes and read his mother's lips.

"It was strange," she said. "The morning after you left, he stayed in his hut, refusing to take anything but water. Rosa told me that he sang songs of protection for you for much of the day. She stopped by that afternoon to check on him. By then it was very quiet. It was as though her grandfather had left and gone someplace else. But his body was still sitting in the room. Worried, Rosa said that she went to check his pulse. Francisco José's eyes flew open when she touched him. It almost scared her out of a year's growth, she said. 'Grandfather, are you all right?' she asked. 'Can I bring you some food and water?' 'No,' he answered. 'Summon the council and bring wood for the fire,' he said. So, of course, Rosa, being a good girl and devoted to her grandfather, she ran and told the others what he said.

"They all came, of course, and sat with him. He shared incredible visions with them, she said. He spoke throughout the night, and he didn't sleep even a wink. Rosa told me that her grandfather got stronger as the night wore on, even when the rest grew tired. But when the morning sun began to light the sky, he fell silent.

"Still he continued through the second day without any food and with little rest. Once again, Rosa came back to check on him. This time she spoke out first. He told her to tell the others to return that night and to bring more wood. He shared his visions with the elders throughout the second night with scarcely a pause. It was daybreak when they went home. And so it went for the third day and into the third night.

"Rosa was concerned for her grandfather, but he told her that he had never felt stronger and that she should go home for breakfast. She went home to get him food, hoping that he was ready to eat. But Francisco José was not there when she got back. He had vanished into thin air. Only his clothes and the necklace of the jaguar claws were left where he had sat. No one saw him leave the village. But Rosa told me that she saw a condor that circled overhead later that day. She said that it was her grandfather letting her know that he would always keep watch over her. That's what she said, and I'm sure she's right."

Juan had to know the truth about her and Don Francisco. Before he could ask any questions, Wilhelmita blew her nose and stood up. She hung her apron by the door, picked up her hoe, and walked out into the garden behind the house. He jumped up and followed her outside. She sunk the metal head of her heavy hoe into the black earth, loosening the soil around the corn stalks. He waved his hand to catch her attention before she lifted the hoe a second time.

"I have something that I want to ask you," he said.

She leaned on her hoe and searched his face. A long silence followed before she nodded. "Go ahead," she said.

He moved his lips carefully when he spoke. "I know that you and Don Francisco were close friends. What was the gift that he saw in you?"

"It was the animals," she said. "He had seen how they responded to me. They trusted and understood me in a way that fascinated him. It was hard to explain to others how I talked without words. I've been asked this many times by those who do not understand the world of the deaf. Francisco José understood."

"I understand,"

"Do you, my son? Do you really know what it's like not to know the sound of your own voice, unable to hear the words of others spoken behind you, and to see people's eyes contradicting the very words formed by their lips? Even when no one else heard me, Francisco José did. We shared a common language. It was a language without words," she said, her singsong voice breaking.

Juan touched her face. "But I know this language without words. It's a language of vibration. At first, on the way to Ausangate, I didn't know what was happening. I would hear or feel a high-pitched or a low-pitched vibration or both, and then I would hear voices or see a vision. I wondered if I had lost my mind. There was the hummingbird and the serpent and then the jaguar before the condor that..."

His mother looked at him with puzzled look, and then her lips spread across her teeth. She covered her mouth, and her belly began to shake. She dropped the hoe and hugged him. "Yes, my son. I can see that you understand. It is what I call the 'noisy silence of the deaf.' It is not nearly as quiet as some might think," she said. She squeezed with the strength of a mother who believed in him even when he couldn't. "How long I have waited for this day," Wilhelmita said. "It makes my heart glad to know that my son lives inside this man. I am happy for you and for me."

She wiped her face with the top layer of her wool skirt and picked her hoe back up. The white fringe on her hat bobbed with the steady swing that brought order to the black earth. He watched her move from one row to the next, humming a tuneless song. Juan waited until she had passed him before he touched her arm. His mother jumped. "What is it?" she asked.

"Before I left the village to go to the mountain, Don Francisco gave me a claw from his necklace. I saw his hand when he held it out to me," Juan said. "It had a scar, just like mine. Don't you think it's strange that he kept this hidden from me until then?"

His mother frowned and waved her hand at him. He touched her shoulder again and waited until she looked up at his lips. Juan softened his words with his eyes. "The puma that came to visit you in the garden was him, wasn't it?"

Wilhelmita held onto the top of the hoe with both hands and let her gaze shift toward the slopes of Inkawari. He followed her eyes. Wind stirred the dust through the village streets and made the figures of men working in the patchwork fields look hazy.

Her gaze drifted to where Maria and Anna were playing. With a deep sigh, she began to speak.

"Francisco José saw how hard I had to work and knew of my stepfather's cruelty to my mother and me. He watched over us, and he brought us food when we had none. After a while, I started to see him more often. We would talk about things, things that he had learned from his teachers. Francisco José taught me the way of changing shapes in dreamtime. I learned how to shift myself into a puma. Together we would run through the highlands at night, playing and exploring in freedom that I could have scarcely imagined.

"One night, when I was older, my stepfather came over to my bed, in a way that was not right. But instead of me, he found a snarling puma waiting in my blankets. He ran out of the house that night, and he never came back. When I told Francisco José about this, he wanted me to become his wife, so that he could take care of me and my mother."

"Did you love him?" Juan asked.

"I was a young woman then, and I was confused. He was much older than me, and I thought of him more like an older brother or an uncle than my sweetheart. His wife had died giving birth. His daughter, Rosa's mother, was almost my age. And I think that sometimes even I was frightened of his powers. His heart was broken when I decided to marry your father instead. After you were born, a puma would come and sit on that knoll when I worked in the garden," said Wilhelmita. She pointed at the rise. "I knew that it was him. He was still watching over me. It would have been improper for us to be together when my husband was working in the fields with the other men. This way we could still enjoy our conversations."

"But Papá found out, didn't he?"

"The other women in the village had begun to gossip. When he heard about the puma, Humberto was furious. He suspected the truth, but he never asked me. He took a stick, and he drove it away. I cried for days afterward, but I knew that it would never come back. Francisco José was a very proud man. After that, he and I rarely had the chance to talk."

Juan furrowed his brow and rubbed the scar in his hand. "Is he...?"

She held her hand up and stopped him. "Only in Spirit, my son, only in Spirit. Francisco José was a good man and a dear friend. I will miss him." Wilhelmita wiped her eyes. "You should go now," she said. "I am sure that you want to spend the day with Rosa, don't you?" The corners of her eyes crinkled upward even as her lips drooped.

He wagged his finger at her. "Some things never change," he said.

Chapter Thirty-Four

Juan pointed to Apu Ausangate, its peaks clad with fresh snow. Standing on the banks of Puma Rimac, he described his trek to Rosa. She worked her tongue along the edge of her chipped tooth when he told her about *Sachamama*. "The serpent spirit is a powerful healer indeed," she said. "I can only imagine how good the hot springs of Pacchanta must have felt. Perhaps we could go there together someday." The twinkle in her eyes made him wonder just how much Rosa had learned about shape-shifting from her grandfather, but he didn't ask.

Her eyes widened when he talked about the farewell visit of the condor. When he handed her one of the wing feathers, Rosa held it to her chest, lightly stroking the edges. "I understand why my grandfather gave you his heart stone and kept vigil without food or rest during your journey," she said. "Your visions were the ones that he shared with us before he crossed over. On the last day, after he had finished teaching and after the others had left, we shared the San Pedro tea and smoked the pipe. I saw you fall from the summit of the sacred mountain, and I wrapped my arms around you, holding on with all my strength."

Her eyes had that faraway look. Juan watched her lips.

"We flew together on the back of Hatun Kuntur in the light that circles the earth," she said. "My grandfather had tears in his eyes when I shared this with him. I had seen the upper world, he said, and you and I would help the people of San Mateo. I would be given a condor feather when it was time for us to work together." She took Juan's hand. Her brown eyes shone like polished copper in the midday light. "I am ready," she said.

They held hands and hiked up the hill that overlooked the village. They scraped out the dirt underneath the gnarled roots of the old *quenoa* tree with papery red bark. Rosa lifted out the remnants of a *mesa* cloth. She took out the rock and cleaned it on the hem of her skirt. It was a triangular stone with a greenish tinge. Embedded with tiny quartz crystals, it was shaped like Ausangate. Juan touched it to his lips.

"This is the stone I found at the stream on my way to the mountain," he said. "I did not expect to see it again."

Rosa had that funny half-smile on her face. "Don't you remember? My grandfather gave it to us when we were five years old. It was to remind us that we would always be together. It was our destiny to fly wingtip to wingtip through life, he said."

"It was your voice that called me back when I fell into that crevasse," Juan said. He traced the outline of her mouth with the stone. The smell of sage scented her hair. He pulled her closer. Her chest softened against his, and he felt the quiver along her back when his lips touched her ear. "You have always known," he whispered. "Together we will soar together as man and wife." He spread out his poncho on the ground for her to sit on. She leaned back against his chest and pulled his arms around her. A gust of wind blew dust funnels across the crest of the hill.

"I have been given my grandfather's home and his herd," she said. "The house is small, and it needs to be fixed up."

"With all of the children we'll have, we will need a lot more room," Juan said.

Rosa dug her elbow into his side. "You need to talk with my parents first before you make so many plans," she said. "Besides you should help Doña Mariana deliver babies, and you would appreciate how much work it takes," she said. "Alicia is having such a time with her baby being late. But she should be delivering any day now."

"When should I talk with your parents?" Juan asked. The thought of asking her father for Rosa's hand in marriage made him nervous.

A smile spread across Rosa's face. "I need to think about it. With my own home and animals, I have many other prospects, you know." She ran laughing down the hill, and he chased her toward the village.

Chapter Thirty-Five

Twin white braids that hung over her stooped shoulders touched the floor when Doña Mariana sat. A solemn look sat heavy on her face. The fire's flickering light lit the opaque eyes that studied Juan with a keen interest. The old woman pushed her straw hat back and pointed at him. Her voice cracked when she spoke. "Juan, we want you to open the circle tonight," she said. Surprised, he stood in the center of the room and took the brown rattle that she handed him.

He summoned the mountains, the plants, the earth, the sun, the moon, the stars, and all sentient beings. He called on Spirit who brought order to creation. When he was done, Juan took the pipe from Doña Mariana and handed it to Rosa. She blew the smoke into the lower, middle and upper worlds and carried the pipe around the circle before she sat down next to him.

With cracks and pops, the burning eucalyptus wood sent sparks flying into the room. Doña Mariana's eyes were closed and her lips were moving. She was talking to someone, but Juan couldn't tell who it was. At last, the old woman nodded her head and looked at him. "Over the past three days, Don Francisco talked much about the path to the sacred mountain," she said. "He shared many things with us, and now he says that you have even more to add."

Juan began on the morning when he had received the blessings of the medicine people. Many sticks of wood were laid on the fire, and the bag of coca was passed several times around the circle. Doña Mariana took the wad of leaves from her mouth and tossed them into the fire when he was finished. She wiped her mouth with the back of her hand.

"I remember Don Francisco's words when he baptized Juan," she said. "He said that although babies stand on our shoulders, they see with new eyes. Children remind us of that which we often forget, that all is truly well with the world. It is their fresh new desires that help to expand creation. They know that they are born of Spirit. It is only us who forget."

Her voice quivered with rising inflection when she pointed at Juan. "You have learned to walk in harmony with Mother Earth," she said. "You have come back to San Mateo with a strong vision." She nodded at Rosa, who tied the necklace of jaguar claws around Juan's neck. "You will need these to go with the one that her grandfather gave you," Doña Mariana said. "This necklace binds you to Rosa tighter than any ropes could. You stand on each other's shoulders now. Soon you will speak to the rest of the village."

The old woman threw a handful of powder into the fire. Sparks flew upward amidst the smoke. The claws grew hot against Juan's chest. He looked at Rosa.

"I see it also," she said. "There is a flame that burns over your heart."

He searched the faces of the elders. Each nodded their approval. His voice trembled when he spoke. "I will tell the people that we are each a gift, a living, breathing gift of Spirit," he said. "That which we believe possible becomes that which we receive. This is the power of *ayni*. What is like unto itself is drawn. We are born free, and it is our dreams that give our freedom wings. When we come into balance with who we are, we become more. We become the gift that we seek.

"Don Francisco told me that San Mateo will change in the years to come when some of our people leave for other places. Each must travel their own journey. But I believe that we can still be an *allyu*, a community of people. It is our heart that makes us who we are, no matter where we live. We need not be afraid of change. The ancestors live inside our bones. Those who have come before have not forgotten us. We must not forget either," he said. "And this is what I will share with the people of San Mateo."

He took a deep breath and realized how hard he had been squeezing Rosa's hand. When he saw the brightness shining in her eyes, he knew that he had spoken his truth.

Doña Mariana visited with him and Rosa after the meeting. "Don Juan, I did not know that you could speak so good with your mouth," she said. "Although the village will listen to you with kind ears, they will want to know if you can bring the rains when it is time to grow potatoes," she laughed.

It was late when they stood in front of Rosa's home. They had taken the long way back through the village. Rosa pointed to the waxing moon. "This is the beginning of a new season for San Mateo," she said.

"Do you think the people will listen to us when it is time for us to speak?" Juan asked.

"Don't worry," Rosa said. "Everything will work out. You'll see." She dropped his hand and pushed the hair from his face. "Go home now and get some sleep," she said. He leaned against her and sought her lips. The door flew open behind them, and they stumbled into the room.

Juan blinked in confusion. Rosa's mother dropped the blankets that she was holding, and her hands flew up to her face. She burst out laughing, and even Rosa's father smiled. When she picked the blankets back up, she pushed them into Rosa's arms. "Alicia is in labor. Doña Mariana is already with her, but she wants you to come too. Hurry, Rosita." Her mother pushed them back out the door and shouted after them. "Tell Alicia that we'll expect to see the baby by morning."

Chapter Thirty-Six

The house was still dark when he opened his eyes. Juan swallowed the anxiousness that rose from his stomach and took a deeper breath. He had dreamed about Marta. Today was the day that he was to stand before the village, she told him. He dressed quickly and folded his blankets, careful not to disturb the rest of the family, still asleep on the other side of the room. It was after he had the fire built that Humberto sat up and rubbed his face. Juan grabbed the empty kettle from the oven and slipped through the door of the stone house.

The stars twinkled in the frigid air. He walked around the perimeter of the corral. The llamas and alpacas snorted when they sniffed at his empty hand. Their breath hung in the dry cold. One of the burros brayed when he scratched it between the ears. With a toss of her head, the cow pushed her calf away from her teats. It picked at a few strands of hay left on the ground. Juan followed the path toward Puma Rimac and thought about the village of San Mateo. It was the people who would decide when he was ready, Don Francisco had told him.

The faint light of dawn touched the crest of Ausangate when he reached the river. A few scattered clouds hung around the lower elevations. The family of torrent ducks paddled past him. The female used her slender, flexible bill to fish for stonefly larvae, while the drake swam beside her. The ducklings fed themselves. Juan filled the kettle and watched his three leaves float downstream. He did what his sister had taught him to do, what his people had always done. He prayed.

He took off his hat and dipped his hand into the water. He touched his fingers to his head, his heart, and his belly. He heard Marta's voice when he put his hand over his heart. *When you were little, you were Mother's ears, and you spoke her words to others.*

Allow Spirit to speak through you in this way. Trust the knowing inside of you. His empty stomach rumbled. It was time to get back, he thought. What would be would be.

The smoke of early morning fires carried the smells of food when Juan walked back to the village. Alicia should have had her baby by now. Of course, Rosa would insist that they help Doña Mariana with the baptism. A little boy and his big sister smiled shyly on their way to fill their kettle. He had no sooner said good morning when a scream broke through the usual stirrings of people and their animals. Several villagers stepped out from their homes. "What's going on?" they asked each other.

"I don't know," one man replied. "It sounded like the scream of a puma."

"It was a woman's cry," his wife said.

Rosa ran toward him. Her face was flushed, and she was out of breath. Her eyes looked tired and anxious. It was hard for Juan to hear her above the confusion. "Come quickly, please," she said. "It's Alicia. She started labor just before the meeting last night. Her mother tried to help her, but she couldn't deliver the baby. Alicia's husband came and got Doña Mariana. When I got there, she told me that the cord was wrapped around its neck. We worked through the night, and we finally delivered a baby boy. But he wouldn't take a breath. Doña Mariana said that we were too late. He had gotten stuck in between the worlds for too long and gone back to Spirit. Alicia screamed a fit. It took both her husband and her mother to hold her down. I didn't know what else to do, so I came to get you. Your mother said that you had gone to get water."

A strong hand gripped his arm from behind. Juan spun around. It was his mother. "Go to Alicia and Roberto. You will know what to do. Go quickly," she said. She took the kettle and thrust his *mesa* into his hands. He ran behind Rosa. The neighbors were gathered in front of Alicia's house. Doña Mariana emerged from inside, bent over with her hands gripped around her walking stick. Rosa massaged her back. The old woman grimaced.

"It has been a long night and I have done all that I can do," she said. "I am afraid that the little one will not be able to join our *ayllu*. It is sad. It is their first one. It's a hard thing for the family, especially for the mother. But she is young and she will have others. In time she will understand."

She stared up into Juan's face with a curious look and blinked her eyes a few times. A smile spread across her face, pushing her lips past the wad of coca leaves inside her cheek. "I see that you have come with friends, dear friends. Go in, please. This is for you and Rosa to do," she said.

Confused by Doña Mariana's sudden change of heart, he followed Rosa inside and shut the door behind them. Alicia lay curled in her husband's arms, sobbing. Her mother held the child wrapped in a white blanket. Rosa whispered that Alicia had woven it for her baby's baptism.

Juan and Rosa knelt beside the grandmother. He unfolded his *mesa*, took out the green heart-shaped crystal and blew over it. Rosa looked at him, and he nodded. "Please, let me have the child," she said, reaching out to Alicia's mother. Juan touched his knees to Rosa's, and she laid the baby on its back between them. Its face, the color of pale blue porcelain, looked doll-like. Juan placed the crystal on the infant's chest.

Rosa played her grandfather's flute. Her breath moved through the condor's wing bone in a faint, breathless sort of whistle at first, but it grew louder. It was like the wind blowing across the *altiplano,* down from the summit of the sacred mountain. The claws grew hot around Juan's neck, and the tips dug into his chest. The room filled with shimmering light. Wind gusted through the room, carrying him out across the yellow grasslands of the *altiplano.* Golden brown feathers touched the tips of his outstretched wings. Rosa soared next to him. They circled wingtip to wingtip above the snow-capped peaks. He folded his wings against his body and dove to the transparent blue waters below. Rosa landed beside him on the shore of Otorongo Q'ocha.

A baby boy lay on his back, his tiny arms and legs curled up. The black jaguar stood over him. Shadowy copper-red figures with waist-length black hair and radiant faces circled around them. "It Is Otorongo's child now," Juan whispered. "Those are the spirits that dance in the wind," he said. "They are the ancestors."

"I know," Rosa murmured. "And the beautiful girl that talks to the jaguar…it that your sister?"

"It is me, dear friend. You and Juanito fly well together," Marta said.

Rosa beamed. "What will happen with the baby?" she asked.

"The jaguar was about to carry the child across the lagoon, but it stopped when it heard the flute," Marta said.

"Is it too late for us to take the boy back to his family?" asked Rosa.

"It would be difficult," Marta said. "Is this is what the family wants?"

"Of course they want him back. More than anything," Rosa said.

Rosa looked at Juan. He saw the light in her eyes. She believed it was possible, and he wanted to tell her that it was. But they weren't Don Francisco. That baby had never taken its first breath. That jaguar was ready to carry the boy across the lagoon. Otorongo sniffed the infant's head with a tender touch of its broad nose. It looked up at Juan. The jaguar's eyes beckoned him closer. *Abandon yourself to possibilities beyond your comprehension*, he heard. *With Spirit all things are possible.* The jaguar blinked, and Juan saw the little boy running ahead of other children along the shores of the lagoon. A crescent moon hung low over the blue waters. Juan nodded, and the jaguar stepped away.

"What is it?" Rosa asked.

"We can bring the boy's spirit back into his body," he said. "But we must hurry. There's not much time." A gust of wind carried them back inside the smoke-filled room, blowing out the candles. A dim yellow aura surrounded the infant.

Rosa swept a condor feather over the baby with brisk strokes. She misted *agua de florida* from his head to his feet three times and three times from his feet to his head. Light flowed in waves over him. Still he lay motionless. Juan felt the eyes of the family on him and Rosa. Alicia was crying again. Rosa picked up her flute. The clear notes that filled the room were the ones her grandfather had played the night her life had hung in the balance. The jaguar claws grew hot around Juan's neck. He touched the heart-shaped crystal on the baby's chest.

"The ancestors watch over their children," he sang. "They bring them home when they are lost. See the ancient ones dancing in the wind, dancing in the wind. They come from the sacred mountain, dancing in the wind." Light filled the room, gilding the stone walls with a bright yellow gold. His sister Marta stood next to a man with waist-length black hair and eyes dark as charred embers. His eyes twinkled, and a smile creased his broad face when Juan and then Rosa recognized him. It was Don Francisco.

Life is an unending river, he said. *Death is what you imagine it to be. When you see through the eyes of Source, all things are possible.*

Juan nestled his fingertips beneath the baby's head. "Rosa, hold his heels and pull ever so gently with the curve of the crescent moon," he said. "Hold them until you feel energy flowing through him like the waters of Puma Rimac." Juan's hands vibrated with two different rhythms, one slower and the other more rapid. The vibrations merged into one. His hands grew warm and a tingly sensation moved up his arms. Rosa nodded. She and Juan took their hands off the child. A golden aura pulsed around the infant.

The tips of Juan's fingers lighted like butterflies on the baby's chest. The delicate ribs trembled with an almost imperceptible vibration. When the infant's face wrinkled and its mouth opened, Alicia's mother shook Rosa's shoulder and pointed. "Look," she said. "My grandson took a breath." Juan looked at Rosa. Her cinnamon brown eyes shone with light. A crooked smile spread across her face when the baby began to cry. She took the crystal from his chest and wrapped him in his white baptismal blanket. The grandmother took the boy and held him up to her daughter. Alicia clutched her son against her breast and kissed his head, crying and laughing at the same time.

Her husband Roberto hugged Juan and Rosa. "Thank you my friends," he said.

When Juan and Rosa stepped out through the doorway of the family's home, an uncertain silence stilled the anxious voices of the gathered villagers. Juan saw his family in the back. Humberto stood with his arm around Wilhelmita. They both held him with their eyes. José, standing between Maria and Anna, held them each by the hand. His sisters waved at Juan and Rosa. An iridescent green hummingbird trimmed in purple hovered over his family before it darted off on wings that sparkled in the sunlight.

Juan exaggerated the movement of his lips so that his mother could see them. "People of San Mateo," he said, "Spirit once again has found a home in our village for a new baby. He is a fine, healthy boy, and his mother nurses him as we speak. The parents want him to be baptized within the weeks ahead. They have asked Rosa and me to perform the ceremony, with your permission, of course," Juan said to Doña Mariana. The elfin woman's head bobbed with enthusiasm.

Rosa squeezed his hand. "And his parents have asked that we choose his name. We agree that his name will be Francisco José. My grandfather would be proud to have his name carried on by this child. The boy will become a great shaman. The spirit of the jaguar is strong in him," she said.

The people erupted into cheers and crowded around Juan and Rosa. The morning sun shone brightly on a pair of Andean eagles that soared over the village, their cries echoing across the *altiplano.*

Acknowledgements

If it takes a village to raise a child, then this book is such a child. *Gift of the Jaguar* is a dream nurtured through the love and encouragement of many friends, family members, colleagues, and teachers. And it owes much to the magnificent people of Peru. Their joy, their hopes, and their dreams for their children inspired us to write this story. We believe that the diverse Andean communities are important to explore not only for their rich culture, but to understand a tradition that honors the environment to promote the well-being of its people. *Ayni,* or reciprocity, is at the heart of an ancient knowledge that speaks of an ethical relationship with nature based on balance and harmony.

We especially appreciate our friend and mentor, Dr. Theo Paredes. Don Theo is a masterful guide into the world of Andean mysticism and plant medicine. Through the programs of his non-profit institute *Poqen Kanchay,* "The Place Where Light Germinates," Dr. Paredes has been a tireless advocate for the restoration of the archeological sites of Peru and for the preservation of the traditional lifestyle of rural communities. With him and José "Pepe" Arancibia we have enjoyed countless adventures and introduced health care practitioners and others to the healing traditions of Peru. And we are grateful to all of these companions on our journeys.

We have been privileged to work with a number of distinguished healers and teachers both in this country and in Peru. Dr. Alberto Villoldo first introduced us to the wisdom traditions of the shamanic arts and was our guide on a number of memorable trips to Peru. We were fortunate to study with Americo Yabar, Juan Nunez Del Prado, and other renowned Peruvian healers and teachers. Our travels with Don Manuel Q'espi, Don Mariano, Don José Q'espi, Don Julian, and others of

215

the *Q'ero* Nation were a great resource to create an authentic feel for the main characters in *Gift of the Jaguar*.

Inlaid within *Gift of the Jaguar* is a younger but equally profound healing tradition of Zero Balancing. Zero Balancing is a system of body work that balances body energy through conscious touch at the level of bone. The founder, Dr. Fritz Frederick Smith, is an osteopath and a master of acupuncture with over forty years of clinical experience exploring the realm of the body-mind interface. It is "Fritz" who inspired us to share our love for Peru and its healing traditions with Zero Balancers and other health care practitioners. Both a friend and mentor, this energetic eighty-year-old man showed us how to ride a zip line through the canopy of the Amazon rainforest in a driving rain. And we deeply appreciate all of our Zero Balancing family, true lights in the world of healing.

We also appreciate practitioners of the *Feldenkrais* Method. With the embodied vision of Moshe Feldenkrais, his students and teachers work tirelessly to expand the frontiers of human potential in lessons of *Functional Integration* and *Awareness through Movement* classes. A special thanks to John's classmates and teachers in his Santa Fe training for their support and friendship.

The Esalen Institute and School of Massage Therapy provided a magical space to germinate our dream "to take a thousand of our closest friends to Peru, fifteen at a time." We love the teachers and massage therapists that keep Esalen on the leading edge of body-mind exploration.

We appreciate the seminal research and programs on human consciousness at the Monroe Institute that also inspired our exploration into well-being.

Our introduction to the Seth material through Rick Stack at the Omega Institute was a turning point on our journey. He is a gifted visionary.

We want to especially thank our friends, colleagues, and teachers in the field of veterinary medicine who promote the well-being of our fellow animal inhabitants on earth in so many ways. We were blessed in our veterinary practice with staff, clients, and patients who appreciated the value of the human-animal bond. Our two Labrador retrievers and two cats continue to be some of our greatest teachers.

Integral to the spiritual and the emotional essence of *Gift of the Jaguar* are the workshops, tapes, and books of Jerry and Esther Hicks. We continue to be inspired by the teachings of Abraham. With masterful insight and wisdom, they have given us practical tools to interweave our experiences in Peru with a profound understanding of the Law of Attraction with the Science of Deliberate Creation and the Art of Allowing.

We have a special appreciation for those clients who come to our practice with a strong desire to feel better. Your journey into wellness and your discovery of the gift that you are is an important theme in *Gift of the Jaguar.*

There is the inspiration for writing, and there is the craft of writing. To turn an idea or a feeling into a full-length book is co-creation at its finest. The dream to write a book was created on a cliff that overlooked the Copper Canyon in northwestern Mexico. It lay dormant until awakened by Susan Ida Smith, a teacher of Zero Balancing. It grew into a manuscript with the support and encouragement of our dear friends in the Zero Balancing community. Your pyramid of support allowed *Gift of the Jaguar* to go into the world and share the message of well-being that your work embodies.

The first draft came to life through the inspired and untiring vision of Alice Austin, a gifted writer in her own right. Every aspiring writer should have a midwife like her to guide them from "an outline" to a story with a message that the reader can understand and enjoy.

Dr. James Peterson, Writer in Residence at Randolph College, created an exclusive honors writing program for John within the confines of his living room and from the largess of his passion for teaching others how to create beauty through the written word. He held *Gift of the Jaguar* to a high standard with his line-by-line editing of the final version. We appreciate Jim and Harriet Peterson for their inspired input on the cover and Jon Roark for his addition to the brilliant design created by Dan Tetrault.

Key improvements to *Gift of the Jaguar* in the early stages came from suggestions made by Betty and Bruce Harrelson. *Reading Like a Writer* by Francine Prose, also their gift, provided keen insight into what makes good writing. Judy Franklin provided editorial services and constant sisterly support. Dory Domanoski not only edited, but she asked the important question in the midst of a workshop that every stalled writer should hear: "Whatever happened to your book?"

Authors Dr. Clarissa Pinkola Estes, Roger Housden, and Patty Summers provided timely emails of encouragement and granted generous permission to use their names to contact literary agents and editors.

We thank all of our family and friends who are not mentioned by name here. You have no idea how important you are to us. We fill endless moments in our heads with thoughts of appreciation for you every day.

A special thanks to the founders and distributors of *XanGo* for your charitable work in Peru and around the world with Operation Kids and XanGo Goodness Meal Packs. We appreciate your vision for the well-being of the earth and all her children.

And finally, to all the wonderful people at Booksurge. Every first-time writer should have people like you to shepherd their book through the process of publishing. To Gaines Hill, our publishing consultant; Sandy Shalton, our editorial liaison; Renee Johnson, our editor; Julian Simmons, and all of our account, design, and marketing teams, a big thank you for manifesting our dream of *Gift of the Jaguar* into reality.

John and Sharon Franklin
May 5, 2009

Appendix

To learn more about John and Sharon Franklin's adventure trips to Peru, *Gift of the Jaguar*, and their healing practices, you can visit their website www.doctorsjohnandsharon.com and www.GiftoftheJaguar.com.

To learn about John and Sharon's holistic nutritional health products business, see www.AllowWellBeing.com.

For more about Dr. Paredes and the Poqen Kanchay Foundation, visit www.pkcusco.org.

To learn more about Dr. Fritz Frederick Smith and Zero Balancing and how to experience "the curve of the crescent moon," go to www.ZeroBalancing.com.

For more information about the Feldenkrais Method, visit www. Feldenkrais.com.

For more information about Esalen, visit www.Esalen.org. To learn more about the Monroe Institute, go to www.monroeinstitute.org and for the Omega Institute see www.eomega.org.

For more about Jerry and Ester Hicks and Abraham, go to www.Abraham-Hicks.com.

Disclaimer

This is a work of fiction. The characters, conversations, and events are the product of the authors' imagination. Our appreciation for the peoples of Peru, their culture, and their traditional way of life is authentic. Any errors in the book are ours alone.

Made in the USA
Lexington, KY
03 April 2010